CAMPUS POLITICS

WHAT EVERYONE NEEDS TO KNOW®

CAMPUS POLITICS

WHAT EVERYONE NEEDS TO KNOW®

JONATHAN ZIMMERMAN

OXFORD
UNIVERSITY PRESS

OXFORD
UNIVERSITY PRESS

Oxford University Press is a department of the University of Oxford.
It furthers the University's objective of excellence in research, scholarship,
and education by publishing worldwide. Oxford is a registered
trademark of Oxford University Press in
the UK and certain other countries.

"What Everyone Needs to Know" is a registered trademark of
Oxford University Press.

Published in the United States of America by Oxford University Press
198 Madison Avenue, New York, NY 10016, United States of America.

Library of Congress Cataloging-in-Publication Data
Names: Zimmerman, Jonathan, 1961–
Title: Campus politics : what everyone needs to know /
Jonathan Zimmerman.
Description: New York, NY : Oxford University Press, 2016. |
Series: What everyone needs to know |
Includes bibliographical references and index.
Identifiers: LCCN 2016010262 (print) | LCCN 2016022737 (ebook) |
ISBN 9780190627393 (hardcover : alk. paper) |
ISBN 9780190627409 (pbk. : alk. paper) | ISBN 9780190627416 (Updf) |
ISBN 9780190627423 (Epub)
Subjects: LCSH: Education, Higher—Political aspects—United States. |
College students—Political activity—United States. |
College teachers—Political activity—United States. |
Academic freedom—United States. | Political correctness—United States.
Classification: LCC LC173 .Z55 2016 (print) | LCC LC173 (ebook) |
DDC 378.00973—dc23
LC record available at https://lccn.loc.gov/2016010262

1 3 5 7 9 8 6 4 2
Paperback printed by R.R. Donnelley, United States of America
Hardback printed by Bridgeport National Bindery, Inc.,
United States of America

For Susan again, and always

CONTENTS

CAMPUS POLITICS

WHAT EVERYONE NEEDS TO KNOW®

INTRODUCTION

MAKING SENSE OF CAMPUS POLITICS

In November 2015, America's college campuses witnessed one of the sharpest bursts of student protest since the 1960s. An email about racially offensive Halloween costumes at Yale sparked an angry confrontation between African American students and a white house master, which was viewed over half a million times on YouTube in the ensuing month. At Claremont McKenna College outside of Los Angeles, another email by a dean—expressing sympathy for minority students who might not "fit the CMC mold"—led to protests about her use of that phrase, culminating in the dean's resignation several days later. Students at Princeton staged a sit-in to demand that the school rename buildings currently dedicated to the Virginia-born segregationist Woodrow Wilson, the former president of both Princeton and the United States. Most remarkably, the University of Missouri's president stepped down following demonstrations against his alleged insensitivity to racism at the school. He also faced a threatened boycott by the football team, which could have cost the university millions of dollars.

Dozens of other campuses experienced student demonstrations as well as university-sponsored "listening sessions," where stone-faced administrators heard their institutions denounced as racist, bigoted, and prejudiced. Overwhelmingly liberal in their own politics, many university leaders seem to have been caught unaware by the volume and vituperation of the protests. Hadn't they bent over backwards to "diversify" their campuses, doing everything in their power to recruit minority faculty and students? And didn't the universities' multicultural coursework and programming demonstrate their good-faith efforts at "inclusion" of minority concerns and perspectives? Beyond the college gates, meanwhile, right-wing commentators had a field day mocking the protesters as coddled children seeking refuge from intellectual (as opposed to racial) diversity. Since the the 1960s, conservatives said, universities had been transmuted from bastions of free speech into islands of "political correctness." So students lacked both the inclination and skill to engage with different ideas; instead, they simply shouted down their opponents in an effort to reinscribe left-wing orthodoxies.

As always, both narratives contained elements of accuracy as well as exaggeration. Student bodies and faculties obviously contain many more minorities than they did during most of our history, when university admission was restricted almost entirely to white Protestants. Likewise, many colleges have added "global" or "multicultural" course requirements and have made notable efforts to infuse the wider curriculum with minority voices. But the fraction of black and Latino students has actually declined at some colleges in recent years, thanks in part to state measures limiting race-based affirmative action in admissions. And minority students continue to report hostile experiences on campus, ranging from outright racial slurs and threats to subtler "microaggressions." Meanwhile, conservatives are certainly correct in asserting that university faculties are dominated by people on the left side of the political spectrum. But professors are hardly the wild-eyed

Marxists that right-wingers often imagine; their sensibilities are liberal but decidedly moderate, as a host of recent surveys confirm. Nor is it clear that they routinely impose their ideological preferences on unsuspecting youngsters, as conservatives also charge. Rewarded mainly for their grants and publications rather than for teaching, professors often pay more attention to their own research agendas than they do to their students. And the students return the favor, devoting a declining fraction of their time to their classes. Indeed, the charge of political indoctrination implies more investment in the academic learning process than either professors or students typically evince.

Upon closer inspection, then, campus politics turn out to be much more diverse—and much more complicated—than the PC stereotype would suggest. Nor have all of the controversies at our universities focused on "diversity," which was the central theme of the November 2015 protests. Especially since 2011, when the federal government instructed colleges to tighten their sexual-assault policies, debates surrounding rape and sexual violence have seized many college campuses. Other students have protested skyrocketing tuition costs and debt burdens, most notably during the 2008 economic recession and again during the 2011 "Occupy" movement. Still others have raised questions about university actions in the broader community, belying the oft-repeated stereotype of young Americans as whiny narcissists who worry only about themselves. At hundreds of campuses, students have demanded that their institutions divest from fossil fuel and private prison companies; others have urged universities to boycott or divest from Israel, unleashing waves of counter protests as well. During the November 2015 demonstrations, indeed, over one-quarter of published student demands included matters that did not directly touch on student life or conditions. Several groups of protesters called on universities to raise wages for custodial staff and other workers, while others demanded that their institutions provide services to needy citizens in adjoining neighborhoods.

But race on campus has surely become the dominant political issue at American universities, as the November 2015 protests and their aftermath confirmed. The most obvious reason lies in the continued underrepresentation of blacks and Hispanics, among both students and professors. Half of published demands in 2015 called on institutions to admit more students of color, while 79 percent demanded the hiring of more minorities on the faculty. Significantly however, an even higher proportion than that—a whopping 88 percent—called for improvements in the racial *climate* of American campuses, not just in their so-called diversity. Students frequently demanded compulsory sensitivity training for the overwhelmingly white faculty, who were accused both of neglecting minority issues and of singling out minorities: some professors simply ignored the question of race, while others reflexively called on students of color whenever it arose. Protesters also asked their institutions to require new courses or trainings for their fellow students, particularly for those who had behaved in allegedly bigoted or insensitive ways. At Amherst, for example, protesters called for mandatory training in "racial and cultural competency" for counter protesters who had put up posters declaring that "Free Speech" was the "true victim" of campus demonstrations that fall. Students on other campuses demanded even stronger measures, including dismissal of faculty who "perpetuate hate speech that threatens the safety of students of color," as protesters at Duke resolved. They also called on the university to hire more minority professionals at its counseling center and to include "mental health trauma ... arising from racial incidents on campus" among the "incapacitations" that can excuse students from attending class.[1]

These examples point to two other important trends in campus politics: a sharp increase in attention to students' psychological health and a somewhat diminished concern—sometimes bordering on outright skepticism—about the right to free speech. To be sure, as we'll see in Chapter 6, minority students have decried the effects of racism on their mental health since the university protests of the 1960s. But recent years have witnessed a dramatic surge in claims of psychological distress, as the November 2015 demonstrations and listening sessions richly illustrated. African Americans, especially, said that racial prejudice on campus had devastated their personal lives. Students spoke of being unable to eat, sleep, or study; others reported that they could only function well among members of their own race, because it was too exhausting—and, sometimes, too traumatizing—to interact with others. Psychological language and argument suffuse student politics today, from complaints about subtle microaggressions to demands for in-class "trigger warnings" about potentially injurious subjects. In part, these developments reflected rising levels of awareness about mental health in American culture and society writ large. But they also embodied a distinct conception of racism—and of other forms of discrimination—as threats to personal well-being. Earlier generations of protesters often rooted their claims in social effects and injustices: racism prevented blacks from living in majority-white communities, for example, while sexism kept women out of certain professions. But today's students typically emphasize the effects of prejudice on *them*, particularly on their supposedly fragile psyches. As one Boston University student wrote, a few months before the November 2015 demonstrations, minorities on campus experience "psychological trauma" on a daily basis. So do women, other students added, particularly when talk turns to sexual coercion and violence.[2]

It's hardly surprising, then, that some students also aimed to limit the kinds of talk and speech that take place at our universities. Admittedly, student politics has always contained a censorious streak: in the Vietnam era, for example, protesters routinely shouted down pro war speakers and also blocked defense-related job recruiters from campus. But the increased psychologizing of campus politics—that is, the framing of issues in terms of their harm to individual minds—has surely multiplied the challenges to free speech, precisely because so many different words, images, and gestures are seen as potentially harmful. Furthermore, as Harvard professor Randall Kennedy recently argued, the renewed emphasis on mental injury has made it more likely that students will *feel* injured in the first place. Writing a few days after photographs of African American law professors at Harvard (including Kennedy's) were defaced with black tape, creating a huge contretemps among students of color, Kennedy chided them for assuming that the act was racist in intent; the vandals could have been protesting the alleged muzzling of black voices on campus, or simply attempting to raise general awareness of racism. And even if the defacement of the photos was a deliberately racist provocation, Kennedy added, he didn't believe that it would scar him—or anybody else—in a deep or irrevocable way. "Some activists seem to have learned that invoking the rhetoric of trauma is an effective way of hooking into the consciences of solicitous authorities," he wrote. "In the long run, though, reformers harm themselves by nurturing an inflated sense of victimization."[3]

Here Kennedy entered a long-standing but often-muffled debate about racism on campus. Was it a constant scourge that required vigilant policing, including speech codes and other restrictions on expression? Or was it more like a periodic annoyance, which activists sometimes inflated in their well-meaning but ill-considered efforts to combat it? Yet even this debate—such as it was—remained constricted by psychological idioms, which prevented a full and free exploration of it. After all, how can you argue with someone who feels pained or traumatized? Won't you actually reinforce a victim's pain and trauma if you raise questions about it? In this environment, doubting any single allegation of racism can become a racist act. Even testaments to racial tolerance and harmony can be received as indirect confirmations of prejudice and bigotry, as Purdue University president (and former Indiana governor) Mitch Daniels discovered during the November 2015 student protests. In the first of their 13 demands, Purdue students called on Daniels to apologize for claiming that the racial climate at Purdue stood in "proud contrast" to that of Missouri and Yale. Protesters insisted that his comment reflected an "erasure of the experiences of students of color," who face a "hostile environment caused by hateful and ignorant discrimination on Purdue's campus." Likewise, anyone who raised doubts about an accusation of sexual assault risked being vilified for re traumatizing the victim in the case as well as every other survivor of sexual violence. Indeed, it seemed, the only proper and good-hearted response to any charge of discrimination or violence was to "validate" it, to use another favored psychological metaphor of our time. Anything less would be "denial," which compounded racism and sexism by turning a blind eye to them.[4]

Student protesters have also found a friendly ear among university administrators, which represents another relatively new trend. For most of our history, the people who run our campuses have been at sharp loggerheads with the students who engage in campus protest. In the nineteenth century, university leaders typically crushed any hint of student disobedience or rebellion—including protests against dining-hall food—with an iron fist. And into the 1960s and 1970s, many leading figures in higher education warned that student protesters at American universities represented an existential threat to the university itself. Right up until his death, indeed, former University of California president Clark Kerr insisted that Mario Savio—the leader of the 1964 Free Speech movement at Berkeley—was a "university hater" who "loathed" the institution. It's simply impossible to imagine any university leader dismissing student protesters in that fashion today. To the contrary, as we saw in November 2015, administrators embraced the demonstrators with explicitly open arms and avowedly open hearts. "We failed you," Yale's president told student protesters. "We have to do a better job." In no instance did a prominent college leader take issue with the protesters; instead, every president and dean dutifully lined up behind them.[5]

To critics outside of the university, the new student–administrator alliance represented a renewed threat to free speech. As we'll see in Chapter 3, black student complaints about racism in the late 1980s led administrators to draft the first campus speech codes; protests by female students brought new policies about sexual harassment, which were also used to restrict speech in certain ways. As administrators embraced another generation of student protesters, some critics feared that new clouds of censorship would gather on the horizon. But the sky wasn't falling on free speech, no matter how many times it was hit. First of all, student protest was mostly limited to a small number of elite private and public colleges; as in prior eras, the vast bulk of American higher education—including community colleges and technical schools—witnessed no unrest at all. For professors, meanwhile, a battered but revamped tradition of academic freedom almost always protected their free speech rights; the very big exception was the growing number of adjunct and contingent faculty, who often lacked the guarantees that the guild provided for full-timers. Even on campuses that did witness protests, finally, most students didn't sound anything like the embittered activists who were quoted in media sound bites about campus politics. In fact, the vast majority of students on campus aren't "political" at all. They come to college to have a good time and—they hope—to get a good job after that. That's bad news, for those of us who care about the diminished civic engagement of young Americans. But it's probably good news for free speech on campus, because there simply aren't enough interested people to provide the ground troops that a real censorship campaign would require.

And if that sounds like faint praise, it should. As we'll see in the ensuing pages, there really *are* serious threats to free speech at our universities: stolen student newspapers, canceled speakers, and—most of all—a campus environment where growing numbers of students and professors say that they self-censor for fear of repercussions. Nobody who cares about the future of higher education should take that lightly. But there are also serious threats to our minority students, whose needs have too often been neglected, dismissed, or ignored. The Yale president wasn't wrong: we have failed them. We need to acknowledge America's ugly racial history and the many ways in which racial prejudice, distortion, and fantasy continue to infect our campuses. But we also need to expose every specific claim of racism—or of sexism, or of anti-Semitism, or of anti gay prejudice—to complete and open discussion, which is the *sine qua non* of the university itself. We should listen to everyone's feelings, of course, but we cannot and must not take them at face value; we should instead investigate and evaluate them, through a full and free exchange of ideas. However imperfectly it has operated in the past, that ideal lies at the heart of the modern academic enterprise. It would be a pity to turn our backs on it now, in a misguided effort to guard against the prejudice and discrimination that still surrounds us.

1

THE POLITICS OF PROFESSORS AND STUDENTS

Are American professors mostly liberal?

Yes. But you knew that already.

What you didn't know, perhaps, is that 43 percent of professors oppose affirmative action for racial minorities in college admissions. And you probably wouldn't have guessed that 44 percent of them disagree with the statement that "business corporations make too much profit," or that 31 percent think that same-sex love is always or sometimes wrong.

So professors aren't the lockstep, party-line lefties that you've read about in the national press. Yes, they vote overwhelmingly Democratic: in the 2004 presidential election, for example, nearly three-quarters of them voted for John Kerry. But that means a quarter of American professors voted for George W. Bush, which might surprise you as well. At my own school, New York University, I didn't have a single colleague in my department who openly supported Bush in either of his national campaigns. But there are over 4,000 institutions of higher learning in the United States, and most of them don't look very much like mine. And some of their professors don't think like me, either.

Nor have professors become vastly more left-wing over time, as another shop-worn media narrative would have us believe. Surveying social scientists in the 1950s, sociologist Paul Lazarsfeld reported that 47 percent identified themselves as Democrats and 16 percent as Republicans; in a broader study of the professoriate in the late 1960s, Everett Ladd and Seymour Martin Lipset found that 46 percent called themselves liberal, 27 percent "middle-of-the-road," and 28 percent conservative. Four decades later, not that much has changed. According to Neil Gross and his colleagues, who conducted our most elaborate study of contemporary professorial politics, 51 percent of faculty call themselves Democrats, 36 percent "independents," and 14 percent Republican. Two-thirds of the self-described independents lean Democrat, which helps explain the resounding support for Kerry and other Democratic candidates. And 62 percent of professors label themselves some brand of "liberal," which does represent a small increase since the 1960s. In 1990, the professoriate was only 11 percent more liberal than the rest of the country; today, that gap has grown to 30 percent.

But fewer than 10 percent of professors call themselves "very liberal" or "radical," belying yet another myth. You've surely read accounts of the (inevitably) bearded radicals of the academy, spouting extremist dogmas from their tenured perches. But real-life radicals (whatever their facial hair) turn out to be in very short supply, and they're heavily concentrated in a small number of fields in the humanities and social sciences. In my own discipline, history, 15 percent of professors self-identify as radicals; in English departments, it's 18 percent. But the real radical redoubt in academia is sociology, where a whopping 38 percent of faculty place themselves in that category. By one estimation, Marxists outnumber Republicans in the discipline by four to one. Radicals are also more frequently found at small liberal arts colleges than at larger research universities or community colleges, where applied fields like business and engineering dominate. And they're mostly middle-career or older scholars, who came of age amid the revolutionary fervor of the 1960s. Radicals are underrepresented among young professors, whose politics are slightly to the right of their elders. The younger generation is predominantly liberal, too. But radical? Almost never.[1]

Why are professors mostly liberal?

Because liberals are smarter. Right?

Wrong. But we do know that smart liberal people are more likely to become professors than smart conservative people are. Some observers have suggested that liberals might be drawn to academia because they value abstract ideals like justice and truth, while conservatives just want to make money. Overall, young people today place a greater accent on financial prosperity and success than prior generations did. But surveys have never revealed a big difference between liberals and conservatives on that measure; indeed, one study of undergraduates showed that self-described political moderates were more likely to prioritize money-making than conservative students were.

So, maybe the culprit is liberalism itself—that is, the liberal bias of those who recruit, select, and promote people within the profession. And that certainly makes some intuitive sense. If you think that liberals are intellectually or morally superior to conservatives, won't you be more likely to pick a left-leaning job candidate over a right-leaning one? In a survey of sociologists, almost half admitted that they would look unfavorably on an evangelical or fundamentalist Christian candidate. And nearly a third said that they'd be less likely to support a job seeker if they knew she or he was a Republican. No wonder that a third of conservative professors in a recent study by Jon Shields and Joshua Dunn said they kept their politics "closeted" until they got tenure. A third of the sample also reported having removed information from their resumes that might "out" them as conservatives, while more than a quarter said they refrained from publishing in well-known right-wing journals for the same reason. Conservative professors use the language of gay American life ("closet," "out") consciously and purposefully: like homosexuals, they say, right-wing professors often have to play along in order to get along. When he was a junior professor, one conservative reported, a senior colleague flatly announced that no Republican would get tenure in his department. The professor bit his tongue until he was tenured, of course. Then he revealed his true politics, at which point several members of the department stopped talking to him. Other "out" conservatives have reported more explicit harassment, including one professor who found a swastika on his office door. It's hard to imagine any academic in this day and age openly admitting a bias against racial minorities on campus, who (as we'll see in later chapters) more often report subtle slights than outright bigotry. By contrast, many faculty feel perfectly free to announce their prejudices against the political minority in their midst.

But that doesn't mean that these biases are what keep conservatives out of the profession. First of all, many conservatives report that they are accepted and even welcomed by their liberal colleagues; mostly mainstream or "establishment" Republicans, conservative professors often feel more comfortable in the quiet, peaceable confines of the liberal academy than they do in hurly-burly GOP of Donald Trump, Ted Cruz, and the Tea Party. Just as Americans condemn Congress but support their own congresspersons, meanwhile, conservatives often say that the broader academy discriminates against right-wingers but their own departments don't. And when we look closely, actual cases of discrimination in hiring and promotion are hard to find.

Only one professor interviewed by Shields and Dunn alleged that his politics had led his department to deny him tenure; but when his provost recognized the same, the decision was reversed. Most of the others reported that their liberal colleagues abided by the merit-driven professional norms of the academy, judging candidates by the quality of their work rather than the content of their politics. Indeed, many conservative professors express a bemused skepticism about media reports that universities are discriminating against conservative professors.

But these reports are all around us, and surely they must play a role in discouraging other conservatives from entering the academy. The right-wing indictment of the left-wing university dates to William F. Buckley Jr.'s bestselling book *God and Man at Yale* (1951), which cast professors as liberal elites (and, in some cases, as communist fellow travelers) who looked down their noses at regular (read: conservative) Americans; a few years later, Buckley famously announced that he would rather be governed by the first 2,000 names in the Boston phone book than by the faculty of Harvard. As we'll see in the next chapter, the campaign received a big boost during the "political correctness" controversies of the late 1980s and early 1990s: to a new generation of right-wing antagonists, the "PC academy" (as they called it) was inimical not just to conservative thought but to knowledge itself. More recently, as political communication has shifted to the Internet, a wide range of right-wing websites have kept up the drumbeat of resentment against universities and the liberals who rule them. Their standard-bearer is FrontPageMag.com, the brainchild of the sixties-radical-turned-conservative-provocateur David Horowitz. Starting in the mid-2000s, Horowitz helped introduce an "Academic Bill of Rights" into 22 state legislatures; ostensibly designed to bring "balance" to the academy, its real goal was to tar universities as citadels of left-wing bias. And it worked. Although none of Horowitz's bills became law, they almost surely influenced public perception of the university. By 2006, 37 percent of Americans agreed that political bias at universities was a "very serious" problem; among Republicans, almost half thought so.

No wonder so few Republicans have decided to enter academia. During the 2012 presidential campaign, GOP candidates Rick Santorum and Newt Gingrich (himself a former history professor) denounced universities as "indoctrination mills" for the Left; the 2016 presidential hopeful Marco Rubio called them "indoctrination camps," which sounded even more sinister. And when another 2016 Republican candidate Ben Carson called for denying federal funding to institutions demonstrating "extreme political bias," none of his listeners had to wonder what kind of bias he had in mind. As we've seen, Republicans aren't wrong about the overall liberal cast of the American professoriate. But professors' politics are much more moderate than the militant radicalism imagined by conservative critics, whose fulminations about ideological imbalance at the university have become a kind of self-fulfilling prophecy. The more that conservatives attack the university, the less attractive it becomes as a career option to members of their own camp.[2]

What are the politics of American college students?

If our universities aim to "indoctrinate" young America into hard-core leftism, they're doing a pretty lousy job of it. American professors are overwhelmingly liberal, but their students aren't; instead, students have hewed closely to larger political trends in American society. And that's been true for a very long time. Although we continue to regard universities of the late 1960s and early 1970s as cauldrons of student radicalism, surveys from the time paint a much more mixed picture: in 1969, at the peak of campus unrest, only 28 percent of American students reported that they had participated in a public rally, protest, or demonstration during their college careers. Two years later, 41 percent of college freshman identified as liberal, 44 percent as "middle of the road," and 15 percent as conservatives. Over the next two decades, as America turned right, so did American students; for a brief moment in the early 1980s, following the election of Ronald Reagan, conservative students actually inched ahead of liberals by 22 to 21 percent. The biggest gain was among moderates, who grew to 57 percent of the student body. They started to decline after 2000, echoing the overall polarization of national politics. Self-described moderates are still the largest category on American campuses; liberals are second and conservatives are third, but both have grown steadily as the moderates wane.

But when we examine students' opinions on specific issues, they often don't fit our standard conceptions of "liberal" and "conservative" at all. Over half of self-identified liberal students oppose the abolition of capital punishment, 40 percent of them want the government to open more areas for offshore oil drilling, 47 percent say undocumented immigrants should be deported, and 49 percent think that most people in poverty could improve their situation if they tried hard enough. Among students who call themselves conservative, meanwhile, 60 percent favor handgun controls, 49 percent support affirmative action, and 47 percent believe in abortion rights. Whatever their views on domestic issues, students are overwhelmingly isolationist when it comes to foreign affairs. Roughly 60 percent of students have lived or traveled overseas, including about one million who study abroad each year, and over 80 percent of students say they are interested in "global issues." But nearly two-thirds reject the idea that the United States isn't doing enough to assist other countries; about two-thirds also agree that these countries' problems can't be solved by outside aid, and 58 percent say that the United States should focus more on its own problems than on the world's. And in 2011, several years before Donald Trump proposed building a wall along our Mexican border, 42 percent of America's students favored a fence or wall to control illegal immigration.

Most of all, though, college students are disengaged from politics altogether. Like the broader American public, students are deeply dissatisfied with the country and its leaders; only 17 percent of students believe that the nation is "moving in the right direction." But they typically don't believe that political action—by them, or anyone else—can change the country's course. "I don't get all worked up about it," one observer told Richard Arum and Josipa Roksa, in their 2014 study of recent college graduates. "I mean, there's only so much that I could do or someone in charge could do." Not surprisingly, then, most college students do not take the trouble to stay informed about current affairs. Arum and Roksa report that only one-third of recently graduated students read a print or online newspaper each day, while nearly one-third read a newspaper once a month or never. Only 16 percent of the graduates discuss politics frequently with friends or family, while nearly 40 percent do so once a month or never. These figures echo wider trends among Americans in the 18–29 demographic, whose overall level of civic engagement and understanding has plummeted since the 1970s. Only 5 percent of people in this age cohort say that they follow news about national politics "very closely"; not surprisingly, then, younger Americans know significantly less about the subject than their elders do. In 2011, when 43 percent of Americans could name John Boehner as the Speaker of the

House, only 21 percent of Americans under 30 could do so. Even among college students, who are more engaged and informed than the average for their age group, two-thirds did not recognize John Roberts as Chief Justice of the U.S. Supreme Court, and more than half drew a blank on Joseph McCarthy and Mikhail Gorbachev. But only 9 percent were unable to recognize Miley Cyrus. Our students might not know much about politics, but they're experts on pop culture.

Nor do students' politics—or their levels of political engagement—change much during college, despite the recurring conservative claim that universities are indoctrinating them. In a much-quoted 2004 survey by the right-leaning American Council of Trustees and Alumni, roughly two-thirds of students at selective colleges reported that their professors had made negative remarks in class about George W. Bush and positive ones about Bush's Democratic challenger John Kerry. Overall, students said, nearly half of their professors "use the classroom to present their own political views"; most troubling, perhaps, almost one-third of the students felt they had to agree with their professors' politics to get a good grade. But a recent study by Kyle Dodson showed that liberal as well as conservative students who spend time with professors tend to moderate their views during college, while disengaged students move either further left or further right; they're influenced mainly by their peers and the broader political culture, not by their professors. And many students and professors aren't deeply invested in coursework. Rewarded mainly for their grants and publications, American faculty devote an average of just 11 hours per week to teaching, class preparation, grading, and other instruction-related matters. Our students respond accordingly, spending an average of only 13 hours per week on their studies. Most scandalously, one-third of undergraduates report studying less than five hours a week. For all concerned, then, college classes are often too much of an afterthought to affect students' political thought one way or another.[3]

What happened to student protest?

Student protest never went away, of course, as the events of November 2015 reminded us. But it has ebbed and flowed since its heyday in the 1960s and early 1970s, when over half of American campuses witnessed some kind of student protest, rally, or demonstration. Students went on strike at 350 institutions, 215 schools experienced shutdowns, and 16 governors activated National Guard units to quell college uprisings. Protests focused heavily on questions of race—as we'll see in Chapter 3—and also on the war in Vietnam. With the conclusion of that conflict, the percentage of students participating in campus protests declined from its peak of 28 percent in 1969 to 19 percent in 1976. But it rose to 25 percent in the 1990s, when protesters renewed their focus upon race, ethnicity, and sexuality. In California, Proposition 187—which limited undocumented immigrants from accessing public services—sparked demonstrations on several campuses; elsewhere, students organized protests and sit-ins to demand ethnic studies programs and to keep out the Reserve Officer Training Corporation, especially in light of the military's "don't ask, don't tell" policy for gay enlistees. Protest activity declined after that and tended to focus on economic issues like student tuition, which became a central concern during the "Occupy" movement of 2011. Students staged walkouts at 150 institutions and signed pledges to refuse to pay their education-related debt, which topped $1 trillion nationwide by the following year.

But just over a third of students said they were following the Occupy protests "very" or "somewhat" closely.

And whereas a quarter of them said they supported the movement, only 1 percent attended rallies or other events. Many others participated online, which promoted new forms of protest but inhibited older ones. On the one hand, as we saw in November 2015, social media could connect activists across campus—and across the country—with a few clicks of a mouse. On the other, it probably reduced the incentive for students to engage in the kind of face-to-face demonstrations that make institutions sit up and take notice. Moreover, many of today's college students simply lack the wherewithal to participate in any type of campus protest. Forty percent of them are over 25 years old, a quarter are parents, half work at least part-time, and three-quarters live off-campus; for most of them, as one college administrator observed, "[I]t is either put food on the table for your family or go to a march." For many well-to-do students at residential colleges, meanwhile, personal goals and ambitions trump political ones. As we'll see in Chapter 6, our new generation of elite college students is the most careerist—and also the most risk-averse—of any that we've measured. Even protest-oriented students have asked administrators for permission to participate in campus demonstrations and sit-ins, fearing that any public challenge to authority could inhibit their job prospects.

Then there are the conservative students, who also have ideological reasons—not just careerist ones—for eschewing the overwhelmingly left-leaning cast of campus protest. They occasionally stage their own political rallies, which bear an ironic parallel to the guerilla-theater tactics pioneered by rowdier elements of the Left in the 1960s. There's the Affirmative Action Bake Sale, where white students are charged more than minorities; Catch an Illegal Alien Day, in which students marked as illegal immigrants are chased and "captured"; Global Warming Beach Day, featuring suntan oil and beer; and also Conservative Coming Out

Day, where conservative students—borrowing the same metaphors as right-wing professors—urge their ideological brethren to emerge from "the closet." These activities seem to be more common at larger and more impersonal research universities than at smaller liberal arts colleges. But at both types of institutions, many conservative students—again, like conservative faculty—simply keep their opinions to themselves. For professors, as we've seen, that's a smart career move. But for students, it's mostly an effort to avoid the worst fate that a young American can imagine: social ostracism. Being conservative "is almost like belonging to a secret society," one student told Amy J. Binder and Kate Wood, for their study of right-wing students. "I'm sure there's plenty of us out there in reality, but we're just kind of afraid to mention it because it's such a hassle." In a recent survey of students at the University of Colorado, over one-third of Republicans reported feeling "intimidated" to share their ideas in class. Nor do they receive much support from administrators, who show earnest solicitude for ethnic and racial minorities but little concern for political ones. Few conservative students report active hostility from school officials; instead, they complain of a steady barrage of institutional programming about social justice, diversity, and inclusion. The liberals who operate our universities rarely pause to acknowledge that these words might have different meanings, depending on how one sees the world.[4]

2

THE QUESTION OF "POLITICAL CORRECTNESS"

What is political correctness?

Once upon a time, in the mid-1980s, a left-leaning cabal of social engineers captured the American university. And not just the classrooms and faculty lounges, mind you; they took over *minds*, by reshaping the words that we use to communicate with each other. Racial minorities became "people of color," the handicapped were renamed "differently abled," older students were "nontraditional learners," and so on. And even as they imposed the new idioms, ironically, these humorless apparatchiks were busily undermining our traditional faith in language itself. Spouting newfangled theories imported from France, they insisted that all truths were products of the time and especially of the culture that produced them. They even put "truths" in quotation marks! So out with Shakespeare and the other Dead White Men of the traditional humanities, whose allegedly universal verities were exposed as mere vanities. And in with the local, the cultural, and especially the "subaltern," which referred to anyone who was colonized, oppressed, or marginalized by the totalizing discourse of the West.

That's the bleak winter's tale that conservatives told about the academy in the late 1980s and early 1990s, and they gave the story a new name: political correctness. But the term itself was several decades old, originating not with the 1980s Right but with the 1960s Left. In widely circulated English-language editions, Mao Zedong's *Little Red Book* explained "correct" Communist Party or Marxist doctrine on a host of different issues. Yet American leftists invoked the phrase ironically, to tease people who rigidly toed the party line (either the Communists' or someone else's) instead of thinking for themselves. "It was always used in a tone mocking the pieties of our own insular political counterculture, as in 'We *could* stop at McDonald's down the road if you're hungry,' or 'We *could* spend good money to get the television fixed,' etc.—'but it wouldn't be politically correct,'" one veteran of the Left recalled. Twenty years later, the term was picked up by conservatives to connote precisely the grim, inflexible group-think that leftists were mocking. It wasn't just that liberal professors dominated the university or tried to indoctrinate their own political perspective, a complaint that went back to William F. Buckley and the 1950s. It was rather that they imposed a fundamentally *illiberal* dogma, challenging the very essence of the university itself: reason, wisdom, and truth (not "truth"!).

But was there any real truth in this story? Surely linguistic convention changed during these years, as anyone who lived through them can testify. Most definitions of "political correctness" focus on language, emphasizing efforts to replace unkind or offensive terms with more neutral ones. Consider this recent definition of PC, from the *Oxford Advanced Learner's Dictionary*: "The principle of avoiding language and behavior that may offend particular groups of people." Or this, from Merriam-Webster: "Agreeing with the idea that people should be careful to not use language or behave in a way that could offend a particular group of people." Some of us are old enough to remember when male professors called women "girls" in class, or when people of Asian descent were described as "Orientals." During my freshman year of college, in 1979, a physical education instructor taught us to shoot a basketball using a flick of the wrist that he called "the faggy wave." But changes in acceptable language have gone far beyond the race/gender/sexuality triad to encompass a wide range of other groups and issues. Nobody in polite company today would refer to a homeless person as a "bum" or to someone who trades sex for money as a "hooker" or a "whore"; some might even object to the term "prostitute," preferring the less stigmatizing phrase "sex worker." Ditto for terms like "cripple" and "retard," which have been replaced by a whole new vocabulary for describing physical and mental disability. As we'll see in the next chapter, some of the now-offensive terms were banned under campus speech codes that arose in the 1990s. But these official rules were enforced unevenly, if at all. The real stricture on language came from social taboo—that is, from the growing campus consensus that the old words were bad, and that good people shouldn't use them. If that was "political correctness," it worked. And it won.

But other formulations of PC go beyond language and into ideology: it's an effort to inscribe new ways of thinking, not just of talking. And surely the words we choose affect the thoughts we communicate. If you call someone a "bum," for example, you're making a statement about the person's culpability that isn't present in the term "homeless." So one of the earliest definitions of PC, from *Webster's College Dictionary* in 1991, said that political correctness was "marked by or adhering to a typically progressive orthodoxy on issues involving especially race, gender, sexual affinity, or ecology." That's a much broader formulation, referring to active promotion of certain ideas rather than the avoidance of negative words and phrases. And it can also carry a tinge of despotism, conjuring a quasi religious or even statist form of oppression: to one especially jaundiced observer, writing in 1990, PC was nothing less than "liberal fascism." Critics especially objected to the ways that certain allegedly PC forces had injected themselves into the humanities, mainly English and history. In the confusing hall-of-mirrors fashion that characterizes the PC debate, these allegedly oppressive departments were charged with exaggerating the oppressive aspects of the United States in particular and of the West in general. Indeed, humanities professors seemed poised to undermine the humanities— and, with them, the university—altogether.[1]

Why did the early PC controversies focus on the humanities?

The first reason is the most obvious one: the humanities *were* changing. In my own field, history, the profession had long been dominated by middle-class or wealthy white men. And for the most part, they wrote about other middle-class or wealthy white men: presidents, generals, business leaders, and so on. The civil rights movement and the boom in higher education in the 1960s brought growing numbers of working-class, female, and African American scholars into the profession, which occasioned no small amount of hand-wringing on the part of the old guard. In 1962, indeed, the president of the American Historical Association warned that America's "priceless asset of a shared culture" would lose its currency in the hands of these new faculty members. "Many of the younger practitioners of our craft . . . are products of lower-middle-class or foreign origins," he cautioned, "and their emotions not infrequently get in the way of historical reconstructions." In fact, the newcomers added depth and richness to American historical scholarship, bringing a host of formerly neglected actors—women, racial minorities, industrial laborers, and so on—into the national narrative. Some scholars called this approach "History from the Bottom Up," to distinguish it from traditional "top-down" research; others simply labeled it the "New Social History." Outside of American studies, meanwhile, younger historians increasingly focused on regions that their forebears had neglected or ignored: Asia, Africa, and Latin America. To understand the world, they argued, we needed to move our gaze beyond the narrow confines of Europe and the United States.

In English departments, a similar shift was underway. New members of the field brought not just more diverse backgrounds, but different ways of seeing the world. Many of them took particular issue with "the canon," that is, the traditional list of "Great Books" that young Americans were supposed to ingest in high school and college. Why should students read Shakespeare but not, say, Jane Austen or W. E. B. Du Bois? And why should they privilege Western texts—whatever the race and gender of their authors—over works from other parts of the globe? Literature scholars also brought a new theoretical apparatus to their work, often described as "postmodernism," which promoted a deep skepticism about human universals of every kind; invoking French theorists like Jacques Derrida and Michel Foucault, postmodernists saw claims about morality and truth less as testable propositions than as expressions of power. So the proper role of the *au courant* scholar was not to come up with "better" (more detailed, more accurate, more imaginative) interpretations of a given text, but instead to "deconstruct" the text (and its interpreters) as products of a dominant Western discourse. "French theory is like those how-to-tapes guaranteed to make you a real estate millionaire overnight," one skeptical observer wrote. "Gain power by attacking power! Call this number in Paris now!" Whatever its own theoretical blinders and excesses, postmodernism was tailor-made for people who wanted to push Dead White Male authors off their long-standing pedestals.

It also unleashed a panic among conservatives, who rallied to defend Western Civilization from the barbarians at the gates. This wasn't just a matter of liberal academicians propagandizing their own point of view, as per the long-standing right-wing jeremiad; it was an attack on the academy itself, or so its conservative defenders claimed. That's the only way to understand the spate of doomsday books that came out in the late 1980s and 1990s about the American university, with each title more alarming than the next: *Impostors in the Temple, Dictatorship of Virtue, Tenured Radicals,* and so on. The most popular and influential expose was Allan Bloom's *The Closing of the American Mind,* which spent 31 weeks on the *New York Times* bestseller list in 1987. A formerly obscure philosophy professor at the University of Chicago, Bloom warned that American higher education had forsaken its founding purpose: the cultivation of intellectual excellence. Abandoning any pretense of standards, universities had admitted under-qualified minorities; and embracing "the latest Paris fashions," as Bloom wryly wrote, educators had also eroded core curricula and other shared academic requirements. "There is no vision . . . for what an educated human being is," Bloom complained. Most schools substituted a laundry list of distribution electives for the old requirements, leaving students "poking around for courses to take." But that also left them intellectually impoverished, Bloom claimed, without the rigorous grounding that the Western classics had formerly provided.

Part of the appeal of Bloom's book lay in its absurdly overheated rhetoric, including much-quoted passages comparing 1960s student protesters to Nazi youth and the Woodstock festival to a Nuremberg rally. It also indulged in a good deal of nostalgia about the good old days of higher education, which were never quite as rigorous—and certainly not as "classical"—as Bloom imagined. "Western Civ" and "Great Books" courses enjoyed a brief vogue after World War I but declined after World War II, when universities diversified their curricula to service the hordes of new students in their midst. And exposés of weak, disconnected course offerings go back nearly a century. The prominent education writer Abraham Flexner complained in 1930 that too many college classes focused on "practical" subjects like stenography, advertising, or even wrestling instead of English, science, and math; lacking "a sound sense of values," universities had "thoughtlessly and excessively catered to fleeting, transient, and immediate demands," Flexner argued. But whereas Flexner blamed this trend on America's crass money culture and the eagerness of university leaders to capitalize on it, Bloom saw only one culprit: left-wing professors and their French-inflected theories. His own story started and in some ways ended in the 1960s, which he called an "unmitigated disaster" for American higher education; to this day, one of the best predictors of a professor's politics is how she or he describes that era. Bloom was teaching at Cornell in 1969, when gun-toting African American protesters took over a building to protest racism on campus. When officials gave in to most of their demands, Bloom said, they signaled the beginning of the end for everything that he held dear.[2]

So how did we get from the humanities controversy to "PC"?

Allan Bloom's 1987 book didn't use the term "political correctness," which hadn't yet entered the *lingua franca*. Nor was the phrase invoked the following year, when student protests at Stanford led the university to revise its Western Civilization freshman course by adding a few required texts from non-Western sources. In the national media, which eagerly picked up on the story, conservative critics reviled Stanford for abandoning the West's intellectual tradition and for capitulating to the philistine horde. "A great university was brought low by the very forces which modern universities came into being to oppose: ignorance, irrationality, and intimidation," declared Ronald Reagan's Secretary of Education, William Bennett, who had formerly served as head of the National Endowment for the Humanities. Critics fixated upon a brief chant that the Reverend Jesse Jackson had led during the student protests—"Hey hey, ho ho, Western culture's got to go"—while media outlets fanned the flames with articles like "Say Goodbye, Socrates," *Newsweek*'s alarmist account of the Stanford imbroglio. Most readers probably didn't realize that Socrates—and other Western thinkers—remained very much at the center of the class, or that this supposedly venerable course of humanistic study had been instituted at Stanford just eight years earlier. Finally, Allan Bloom himself weighed in on the Stanford controversy through a letter in the *Wall Street Journal*. "Stanford students are to be indoctrinated with ephemeral ideologies," Bloom wrote in 1989, dismissing the non-Western additions to the course. "This total surrender to the present and abandonment of the quest for standards with which to judge it are the very definition of the closing of the American mind, and I could not hope for more stunning confirmation of my thesis."

The following year, amid another burst of national attention, these debates got folded into a new media frame: political correctness. *Newsweek* led the way with a December 1990 cover story, featuring an especially incendiary headline—"Thought Police"—in large, menacingly shadowed block letters. "There's a 'Politically Correct' Way to Talk About Race, Sex and Ideas," the cover declared. "Is This the New Enlightenment—or the New McCarthyism?" Inside, the story left little doubt about the answer. Using the acronym "PC" no fewer than 27 times, it flatly declared that political correctness was a "totalitarian philosophy." Most of all, it linked campaigns to change everyday language with the broader academic challenge to Western-centered scholarship and teaching. "The goal is to eliminate prejudice," the article explained, "not just of the petty sort that shows up on sophomore dorm walls, but the grand prejudice that has ruled American universities since their founding: that the intellectual tradition of Western Europe occupies the central place in the history of civilization." A few weeks later *New York* magazine produced its own cover story, "Are You Politically Correct?," which compared PC "fundamentalists" to fascists and communists as well as to orthodox Christians; lest anyone miss the point, the article was illustrated with pictures of Nazi book-burnings and Red Guards attacking victims in Maoist China. Then came Dinesh D'Souza's *Illiberal Education*, the best-selling book in the doomsday genre since *The Closing of the American Mind*. Published in 1991, on the cusp of the media panic over PC, D'Souza's book referenced the term only once. "It is common in universities today to hear talk of politically correct opinions, or PC for short," Yale dean Donald Kagan said, in an interview D'Souza quoted. "These are questions that are not really open to argument." Indeed, Kagan said, it took "real courage" to challenge them. "I was a student during the days of McCarthy," Kagan told D'Souza, "and there is less freedom now than there was then."

As we'll see in Chapter 4, liberal professors have frequently linked any stricture or pressure they dislike to Senator Joseph McCarthy and his attacks on left-leaning faculty in the 1950s. And many conservatives before the 1980s defended McCarthy, claiming either that his victims got what they deserved or that liberals had exaggerated the degree of the repression he fostered. But the PC debate brought the American Right onto the anti-McCarthy bandwagon, which represented a concession as well as a complaint: admitting that McCarthyism was a bad thing, conservatives insisted that they were the targets of a new form of it. The charge wended its way from academia and the mass media into the upper reaches of the political universe, reaching an apotheosis of sorts with the 1991 commencement address at the University of Michigan by the president of the United States. On the 200th anniversary of the Bill of Rights, George H. W. Bush warned, free speech was "under assault" on our college campuses. "The notion of political correctness has ignited controversy across the land," Bush declared. "And although the movement arises from the laudable desire to sweep away the debris of racism and sexism and hatred, it replaces old prejudice with new ones. It declares certain topics off-limits, certain expression off-limits, even certain gestures off-limits." Unlike some of the more vitriolic accounts of PC in the popular press, Bush was willing to admit that political correctness had sound motives. But it had sacrificed free speech on the altar of racial and gender egalitarianism, putting the entire academic enterprise at peril.[3]

Does political correctness even exist?

One of the many bizarre aspects of the PC debate is that almost nobody readily identifies themselves as politically correct: like body odor or accented speech, it's the kind of thing you only notice in someone else. So it's worth asking if the entire phenomenon might be illusory, a kind of vast right-wing conspiracy to arrest the democratizing trends of the modern university. Conservatives didn't like the fact that universities were opening their doors to more people and more perspectives, the story goes; so they labeled these changes "politically correct," which was a perfect way to discredit them. There's plenty of evidence that conservatives promoted and financed attacks on universities going back to early 1970s, when a memo by future Supreme Court Justice Lewis Powell to the U.S. Chamber of Commerce's Education Committee urged the business community to mount a public relations campaign against ideological "imbalance" in higher education. After that, right-wing think tanks endowed professorships for conservative professors and also funded some of the best-known critics of the university. Dinesh D'Souza got his start at the *Dartmouth Review*, one of several conservative college newspapers endowed by the Institute for Educational Affairs; then he produced *Illiberal Education* with grants from the American Enterprise Institute and the Olin Foundation, which also gave generous financial support to Allan Bloom. In 1989, just before the outbreak of the PC controversy, a former aide to Ronald Reagan told the right-wing Heritage Foundation that conservatives were launching "a counteroffensive on the last Leftist redoubt, the college campus." Political correctness was the fruit of this semi secret labor, some left-wing critics charge, a convenient weapon for conservatives to tar the entire academy with baseless charges of censorship and anti-intellectualism.

But PC had plenty of liberal critics, too, which suggests that it was more than just an invention of the right-wing spin machine. As we'll see in the next chapter, some liberals blasted the speech codes that arose in the late 1980s and early 1990s in response to racist incidents on campus. More commonly, though, they condemned PC for focusing too heavily *on* speech—the right and the wrong kind—and thereby "confusing verbal purification with real social change," as the feminist author Barbara Ehrenreich worried in 1994. Some of the most fervent liberal denunciations of PC came from foreign observers, who linked it to Americans' puritanical streak: only in the United States, they said, would people go to such lengths to cleanse their communities of imagined sin. "We want to create a sort of linguistic Lourdes, where evil and misfortune are dispelled by a dip in the waters of euphemism," wrote Robert Hughes, a pungent Australian chronicler of American life. "Does the cripple rise from his wheelchair, or feel better about being stuck in it, because someone . . . decided that, for official purposes, he was 'physically challenged'?" Other liberals scored PC for promoting facile forms of postmodernism, which likewise inflated the importance of language. Their critique gained national attention in 1996, when the journal *Social Text*—a leading purveyor of postmodern theory—published an article by physicist Alan Sokal, which purported to show that gravity was a "social construct." Sokal then revealed that the article was a hoax, which he had written to remind his fellow liberals about the dangers of confusing words with reality. "Facts and evidence do matter," Sokal warned. "Theorizing about 'the social construction of reality' won't help us find an effective treatment for AIDS or devise strategies for preventing global warming."

Most of all, liberals said, PC spawned an "identity politics" that made it harder for us to communicate—and to cooperate—across our racial and ethnic divides. "In a world of shifting identities, emphasizing one's difference from others can give organizations, and people, a sense of security," wrote Barbara Epstein, a staunchly left-wing critic of political correctness, "but it can also get in the way of efforts to find common ground for action." At the University of California–Santa Cruz, where Epstein taught, PC had put everyone—students, faculty, and staff—on edge; afraid of saying the wrong thing, they often stayed quiet when a controversial subject arose. Epstein could not get her students to discuss books that criticized aspects of the civil rights and feminist movements; if they agreed with the texts, students felt, they might be accused of racism or sexism. At the University of California–Los Angeles, likewise, liberal historian Russell Jacoby found that his students often went mute at the mention of race or gender. The problem lay not in administrative speech restrictions but in the overall climate of the university, which discouraged precisely the conversations that Americans needed to have. "Students do not fear the authorities or the dean . . . but the ridicule of other students," Jacoby wrote in 1994. "Every word or step is charged. Conclusion? Stay mum." Several years after the debate over "Western Civilization" at Stanford, a survey of students at the university found that they, too, mostly avoided discussing race. "I'm scared to be called a racist," one student confessed. "You've really got to be careful all the time." The same went for discussions of gender, even at women's colleges. At Wellesley, nearly a third of students in its women's studies program said they felt "silenced or at risk expressing unpopular opinions" in class. "Students at Wellesley don't want to hear about women who choose more traditional roles such as wife and mother," one student privately complained. "To support such a choice is to be 'politically incorrect.'"[4]

Has the PC debate gone away?

Political correctness was a hot topic in the 1990s, when it first entered our public dialogue. What about PC today? You won't find much controversy surrounding the humanities, which stoked so much furor during the initial PC debate. That's partly because of changes in the curriculum itself, which is far more diverse and multicultural than anything Allan Bloom could have imagined. As the November 2015 protests reminded us, there are plenty of critics who don't think it's diverse or multicultural enough. Significantly, though, you didn't hear anyone on our campuses—on any side of the political spectrum—complain that teaching and learning about nonwhite or non-Western peoples would diminish or overshadow the academy's historic emphasis upon the Western tradition, as Bloom and other conservatives warned. Twenty years after it sparked the first panic over PC, diversity has become a shared objective—arguably, the central objective—in almost all of the humanities.

But the humanities themselves have continued to constrict, which might also explain the reduced debate around them. By 1984, three years before Bloom's book appeared, the number of students majoring in so-called practical or vocational subjects—business, health, education, and so on—topped the total majoring in the liberal arts. And the imbalance has widened even further since then, with the humanities often taking the biggest hit of all. Students vote with their feet, and they're walking away from subjects like history, philosophy, and literature. Working-class students, especially, see the humanities as a luxury they can ill afford: they typically view college as a route to a middle-class job, not as a vehicle for personal exploration and development, so they prefer applied and vocational majors to traditional ones. Several prominent politicians have recently suggested that we reduce or eliminate public subsidies for students in the humanities, precisely because these fields don't lead directly to well-paid work. For the most part, then, we no longer debate what the humanities should teach; instead, we're increasingly asking whether we should teach them at all.

Finally, what about the claim that PC spawns ideological orthodoxy? Is there still a kind of social pressure to conform—or to self-censor—on our campuses, as professors like Epstein and Jacoby reported in the 1990s? Whether you label it "PC" or not, the answer would appear to be yes. In a 2010 study by the American Association of Colleges and

Universities (AACU) asking respondents whether it was "safe to hold unpopular positions on college campuses," only 40 percent of freshmen "strongly" agreed; just 30 percent of seniors strongly agreed, suggesting that the college experience makes our students feel more constricted rather than less so. As an Amherst student wrote in a 2001 essay, "The Silent Classroom," many students "stop talking in class" midway through their freshman year out of fear of saying the wrong thing. Most alarmingly, perhaps, only 16.7 percent of *professors* in the AACU survey strongly agreed that it was safe for them to hold unpopular views. And it's not only conservative faculty who feel that way! As we saw in the previous chapter, almost half of American professors oppose race-based affirmative action in admissions; given the overwhelming liberal cast of the academic profession as a whole, these opponents surely include a healthy dose of left-wingers. Yet you wouldn't know that from listening to our public debate on affirmative action, where the professors who speak up are almost always in favor of it. For the most part, the rest stay quiet. You can choose to call that political correctness, if you'd like (or not). Whatever name we give it, however, it can't be good—for universities or even for affirmative action, which could only benefit from the deep scrutiny of a full scholarly dialogue. As we'll see in the next chapter, there really are some things that can't be said safely at the university. And many people—perhaps, most people—at the university seem OK with that.[5]

3

DIVERSITY AND ITS DISCONTENTS

Have American universities become more diverse?

Of course they have. The number of black college students in the United States tripled between 1976 and 2012; during that span, African Americans went from 9 percent to 14 percent of the undergraduate population. The rise in Hispanic enrollment was even sharper: comprising just 3.3 percent of the student body in 1976, Hispanics rose to 14 percent—the same fraction as African Americans—in 2012. A third of our undergraduates are 25 or older, and a quarter of them are parents. But the most profound change on our campuses over the past half-century has concerned gender, not race or age. After World War II, when veterans flooded into our universities under the G.I. Bill, undergraduate men outnumbered women by more than two to one. But in 1982, for the first time, female students received more college degrees than did males. They have continued to outpace men ever since, inverting the gender gap of prior generations. By 2009, 57 percent of B.A.s were awarded to women.

But American higher education is still marked by huge inequalities, especially when it comes to race. Although African American and Hispanic students represent about a third of America's college students, they make up only

14 percent of students at selective public and private colleges. These schools spend more time on student instruction, have higher graduation rates, send more students to graduate programs, and give alumni a bigger advantage in the job market than other institutions do. Minority students are overrepresented at community colleges and especially at for-profit institutions, which now enroll about half of black and Hispanic students; whereas students at the for-profits pay more tuition and default on their student loans more often than people at other institutions, they also have lower salaries and rates of employment after graduation. That bodes ill for racial minorities in the future, given everything we know about the intergenerational transmission of inequality. The small number of blacks and Hispanics at selective colleges come mostly from the middle and upper classes, and their offspring are likely to share that background. But the vast majority of our minority students attend nonselective institutions, where they're more likely to drop out of college and also to raise children who lack a postsecondary degree.

Finally, recent political campaigns to limit race-based affirmative action have probably increased this gap by inhibiting minority enrollment at the selective institutions. In its landmark *Regents of the University of California v. Bakke* decision in 1978, the Supreme Court ruled that universities could consider applicants' race in order to enhance the diversity of the student body; a quarter-century later, in two 2003 cases involving the University of Michigan, the Court confirmed that schools could include race as part of a broader, "holistic" examination of each candidate. Starting with California's Proposition 209 in 1996, however, six states approved referenda banning race-based affirmative action at public universities. In a seventh state, New Hampshire, the legislature banned it, and in an eighth state, Florida, it was prohibited by an executive order of the governor, Jeb Bush. Universities in several of these states attempted to preserve racial diversity by developing so-called percent plans, which automatically admitted the top graduates from each high school; given the high rate of racial segregation in K–12 education, the plans virtually guaranteed that a subset of minority students would be offered spots at competitive public institutions. Other states added socioeconomic factors such as family income and parents' education level to their admissions formulas; still others increased financial aid opportunities for lower-income students. But it's unlikely that these measures can recruit and retain enough minority students to compensate for the loss of race-based affirmative action. At Berkeley and UCLA, two of California's most competitive public universities, the percentage of black, Hispanic, and Native American students plummeted more that 50 percent after Proposition 209 passed. Their percentiles have trickled up since then, but they still remain below their pre-1996 levels. Controlling for other factors, a 2014 study from the University of Washington confirmed that minority admissions at selective schools are lower in states that banned affirmative action than in ones that didn't.

Some scholars have suggested that this might not be a bad thing for academically disadvantaged minorities, who are more likely to succeed at less competitive schools. That's the crux of the so-called Mismatch Theory put forth by Richard Sander and Stuart Taylor Jr., which was invoked by Justice Antonin Scalia during a 2015 Supreme Court hearing about a challenge to the University of Texas affirmative action policy. "There are those who contend that it does not benefit African-Americans to get them into the University of Texas where they do not do well, as opposed to having them go to a less advanced school, a slower-track school where they do well," Scalia said. The remark drew an outraged reply from Senate Minority

Leader Harry Reid, who bluntly announced that Scalia was trafficking in "racist ideas"; in a more tempered vein, others argued that Sander and Taylor—and, by extension, Scalia—had exaggerated the academic failures suffered by minority students and had underestimated the job market boost they receive from attending a selective school. Significantly, however, nobody questioned the overall objective of increasing minority representation at American universities. Like diversity in the curriculum, a diverse student body has become a shared goal across higher education. Our debates focus mainly on the means to that end, not on the goal itself.

Over these same years, universities have also made substantial efforts to add racial minorities to their faculties. But that task turns out to be even harder than diversifying the student body, which looks much more like the rest of America than university faculties do. In 2013, when about a third of students were black or Hispanic, only 4 percent of full-time professors were black and 3 percent were Hispanic. At some of of our most elite schools—including Harvard, Stanford, and Princeton—there are more faculty from other countries than there are American-born black and Hispanic professors combined. Meanwhile, women comprise just a third of our full-time faculty, even though they make up over half of our college students and also receive half of the Ph.D.s awarded in the United States. By contrast, doctoral degrees conferred to blacks and Hispanics have lagged far behind their respective rates of undergraduate enrollment. In 2013, only 6.4 percent of awarded doctorates went to African Americans. In my own discipline, history, 49 African Americans received Ph.D.s; in math, only 26 did. Two years earlier, the *Journal of Blacks in Higher Education* listed 20 different fields that did not award a *single* doctorate to an African American that year. All told, we are now producing about one new black Ph.D. for every three college campuses in America.[1]

Why did universities become more diverse?

The standard answer is that students in the late 1960s demanded it: inspired by the national civil rights struggle, they staged rallies and sit-ins to compel their institutions to recruit more diverse students and faculty. But the drive for diversity actually began several years before the student protests, spurred by administrators who worried that minorities—particularly blacks—were being denied the opportunities that others enjoyed during America's postwar boom. They also fretted about the fate of elite universities, formerly dominated by slothful sons of alumni but increasingly crowded by hyper-achieving newcomers who cared *too* much about academics. "Sometimes I lie awake nights worrying about whether we've been kidding ourselves into taking a lot of brainy kids who are too egocentric ever to contribute much to society," Yale's admissions dean wrote in 1960; at Brown, likewise, officials worried about an oversupply of "the self-centered student" who placed "his own advancement" over "the well-being of the community." So admissions officers began to seek students who fell outside the traditional elite-college pool, especially minorities. Dozens of schools established summer programs to recruit prospective minority students, who often lacked the educational advantages of other candidates; others designed special programs to assist minorities after they enrolled. By the mid-1960s, the top colleges were already competing for the top minority students. After the 1957 Soviet launch of the Sputnik satellite, which sparked a new search for talented math and science students, colleges had boasted about the average standardized test scores of the classes they admitted. But just a decade later, in 1967, Amherst's admissions director quipped that universities' new "status symbol" was "how many Negroes you get."

Meanwhile, minority students were transforming diversity from an institutional status marker into a moral and political imperative. Although African Americans represented just 6 percent of college students in 1968, they accounted for more than half of the participants in campus protests that year. Their central demand was for universities to recruit and enroll more people like them. At the University of Wisconsin, black students called on the school to admit 500 black students in the fall of 1969; University of Illinois students demanded that blacks make up 10 percent of incoming freshmen; students at Northwestern proclaimed that each admitted class should be 10 to 12 percent black, with half of the African Americans drawn from "inner-city school systems"; and at the University of Washington, the Black Student Union demanded that the school enroll 300 blacks, 200 Native Americans, and 100 Mexican Americans. Following a sit-in by black and Puerto Rican students, the City University of New York (CUNY) established "open admission": if you graduated from a New York high school, you could attend one of the CUNY campuses. And while other large institutions never guaranteed a spot for every applicant, they certainly lowered their test-score benchmarks in order to admit more minorities. Acceding to protesters' demands, Illinois increased its percentage of African American students from 1 to 10 percent in a single year. Yet only 21 of 583 admitted blacks had a combined score of 21 on the American College Testing exam, whereas 90 percent of other freshman did. By their sophomore year, fewer than half of the new African American recruits had a C average or better. Black college enrollment rose nationwide by a remarkable 56 percent between 1970 and 1974, when white student enrollment increased by just 15 percent. But African Americans lagged in achievement, leading to a new round of protests and demands for remedial classes to help black students improve their academic skills.

At the same time, blacks and other minority students were also demanding courses with a different academic focus: the culture and history of minorities themselves. Following a five-month student strike, San Francisco State University established the nation's first Black Studies program in 1968; by the early 1970s, 500 institutions had started some kind of department, degree program, or research center in the area. Many of these efforts were a direct response to student activism; indeed, a single protest by black students on a campus tripled the odds that a Black Studies program would be established there. Other student groups followed suit, demanding programs in Women's Studies, Asian American Studies, Native American Studies, and more. Especially in the early years, some of the "professors" in these new programs lacked traditional academic pedigrees: a course at Cornell on "Black Ideology" was taught by a former civil rights organizer with only two years of college under his belt, while Kent State's class on the "Black Experience" was instructed by a "graduate" of the Ohio Penal System. From the students' perspective, however, the purpose of these courses was not simply to gain another credential. It was to recognize and celebrate their distinctive experience, which was ignored or neglected by the larger institution. Courses in Black Studies would help African Americans retain and develop what was unique to them, advocates said, even as the university seemed determined to blot it out. "We refuse to have our ties to the black community systematically severed; to have our life styles, our ambitions, our visions of our *selves* made to conform solely to any white mold," a group of black students at Vassar declared, in a typical statement.

Most of all, African Americans argued, black-oriented courses and programs would steel them against the ignorance, contempt, and and outright racism that they routinely encountered on campus. At Harvard, where 40 black students entered in 1965, few whites believed they actually attended the school; store clerks refused to accept their checks, and guards persistently asked them for identification. Protesting a similar situation, black students at Columbia told a guard that they would watch him for a half hour to see if he also demanded identification from whites. In class, white professors and students either ignored African Americans or condescended to them by explaining concepts that the black students already understood. And in dormitories and other social settings, blacks frequently faced questions about their dancing ability, their experience in the "ghetto," and other stereotypes. "I came here to be a student, not to educate whites about blacks," one Yale student complained in 1969. "I'm tired of being an unpaid, untenured professor teaching these guys the elementals of humanity."[2]

Why did universities establish speech codes?

The essential premise of the diversity ideal was that a wider array of racial and ethnic groups would enhance tolerance and understanding *across* these groups. That was also the foundation of the *Bakke* decision, where the Supreme Court endorsed affirmative action not to compensate for historic discrimination against racial minorities but to help students of all backgrounds "learn from their differences" and "stimulate one another to re-examine even their most deeply held assumptions about themselves and their world," as the Court declared, quoting the president of Princeton. But the reality of our campuses often told another story, particularly for African Americans. In a survey of black students who had enrolled at the Massachusetts Institute of Technology between 1969 and 1985, three-quarters reported "negative experiences"—especially feelings of alienation and loneliness—from attending a majority-white college. Starting in the mid-1980s, meanwhile, newspapers began to report a troubling rise in overtly racist incidents on campus. After the last game of the 1986 World Series between the Boston Red Sox and the New York Mets, drunken brawls erupted at the University of Massachusetts at Amherst between white Red Sox fans and black Mets supporters; at one point, a mob of 3,000 whites chased black students and beat several of them. The following year, slur-filled handbills declaring "open hunting season" on blacks were distributed at the University of Michigan; at the University of Wisconsin, meanwhile, students paraded in blackface at one fraternity and conducted a mock "slave auction" at another. In retrospect, it was never clear whether racial prejudice and harassment actually spiked during this era; although one organization counted 250 incidents of campus bigotry between 1986 and 1989, nobody knew whether that represented an increase from prior years. Given the overall growth in the college population, moreover, the chance of a racist incident occurring on campus might have gone down even if the raw number of such incidents had risen.

But widespread media reports on these episodes sparked demands for action, especially from minority students. So in 1988, on the heels of its racist-handbill scandal, the University of Michigan enacted the nation's first campus speech code. It barred "any behavior, verbal or physical, that stigmatizes or victimizes an individual on the basis of race, ethnicity, religion, sex, sexual orientation, creed, national origin, ancestry, age, marital status, handicap or Vietnam-era veteran status." The Michigan rule also banned sexual advances and "verbal or physical conduct" that "[c]reates an intimidating, hostile, or demeaning environment" on campus. By 1992 at least 300 universities had adopted speech codes, many of them modeled on the Michigan measure. A 1994 survey of 384 universities found that 60 percent of the institutions had rules banning verbal abuse and harassment, 28 percent barred offensive words or expressions, and 14 percent prohibited speech causing emotional distress. The University of Maryland instructed students to avoid "idle chatter of a sexual nature"; Syracuse's speech code barred "sexually suggestive staring, leering, sounds or gestures"; and at the the University of Connecticut, students were warned against "inappropriately directed laughter." But all of these terms were notoriously slippery, as a federal district court judge wrote in a 1989 ruling that struck down the University of Michigan code. "What one individual might find victimizing or stigmatizing, another individual might not," the judge wrote. Since then, five other federal courts have examined university or municipal speech codes, and in every case the codes were deemed unconstitutional. The biggest blow came from the U.S. Supreme Court, which struck down a St. Paul, Minnesota, ordinance against hate speech in 1992. Under the First Amendment, the Court said, governments can't bar speech simply because they disapprove of its content. By prohibiting expression targeted at certain groups but not at others, that's exactly what the city of St. Paul was doing.

But many universities retained their speech codes or added new ones, even in the face of judicial decisions prohibiting them. According to a 2012 survey of 392 colleges, two-thirds still have speech codes barring expression that courts have found protected under the First Amendment. Rhode Island College declared that it "will not tolerate actions or attitudes that threaten the welfare of any of its members"; the University of Northern Colorado banned "inappropriate jokes"; and my own institution, New York

University, prohibited "insulting, teasing, mocking, degrading or ridiculing another person or group" as well as "inappropriate" comments, questions, and jokes. To be fair, private schools like mine don't face the same constitutional restrictions as public institutions do, because the First Amendment only limits action by the government. But private colleges also like to see themselves as bastions of civil liberty, so they have sometimes been shamed into revising or removing their speech codes. The most embarrassing incident took place in 1993 at the University of Pennsylvania, which charged a student with violating its code after he pleaded with some partying African American sorority members to keep down the noise. "Shut up, you water buffalo," the student shouted. "If you want a party, there's a zoo a mile from here." In his native Israel, the student later explained, the term "water buffalo" referred to a rowdy person, but the black students interpreted it—and his zoo remark—as racial insults. Facing a deluge of mockery in the national press, the University eventually dropped the charges against the student and—two years later—it eliminated its speech code as well.

Other students haven't been so fortunate. In 2003, a student at the University of New Hampshire was found guilty of harassment and disorderly conduct—and of violating the school's affirmative-action policy—for circulating a flyer joking that female students could lose their "freshman 15" by taking the stairs instead of the elevator in his dormitory. Kicked out of the dorm, the student was forced to live out of his car for several weeks; only after Jon Stewart's *Daily Show* expressed interest in his case did the university allow him back inside. In 2004, a student disc jockey at Occidental College was censured for making jokes about his own mother on the air; his remarks disparaged "the category 'mother,'" administrators said, which violated the school's anti harassment policy. Tufts found a conservative student newspaper guilty of racial harassment after it published a satire of Islamic Awareness Week, which noted—correctly—that Saudi women were prohibited from driving and that homosexuality was a capital crime in several Islamic countries. And that same year, most astonishingly, Indiana University found another student guilty of the same charge—racial harassment—for reading a history book entitled *Notre Dame vs. the Klan* in public. It made little difference that the book actually celebrated the trouncing of the KKK in a 1924 street fight with students at Notre Dame; indeed; its subtitle was *How the Fighting Irish Defeated the Ku Klux Klan*. But the book's cover featured a picture of a Klan rally, which could offend onlookers, so Indiana ruled that the student had violated its policy by "openly reading [a] book related to a historically and racially abhorrent subject."

To be sure, some of the students charged with speech-code violations exhibited openly racist behavior. In 2015, the University of South Carolina suspended a student for writing the word "nigger" on a whiteboard in a campus study room. And earlier that year, in an episode that made international headlines, the University of Oklahoma expelled two white students and shut down their fraternity after they led members in a chant boasting that they would never accept a black pledge. "You can hang him from a tree, but he will never sign with me," they sang, captured in a cellphone video that went viral a few days later. But this wasn't the first time that the offending fraternity, Sigma Alpha Epsilon, had found itself in hot water for racist activity. In 1982, the University of Cincinnati suspended its SAE chapter after members held a "trash party" on the eve of Martin Luther King Jr. Day; advertisements for the party encouraged people to bring canceled welfare checks and "a radio bigger than your head." And ten years after that, Texas A&M University fined its own SAE chapter for staging a "jungle fever" party where students wore black-face. What was different in 2015 was the display of the fraternity's bigotry on the Internet, readily viewable by millions of people. So was the involvement of the Oklahoma football team, which staged a protest walk against racism after a prized African American recruit—citing the hateful fraternity video—rescinded his decision to attend the university. Prefiguring the threatened boycott by the University of Missouri team in November 2015, which helped force the resignation of the school's president, the Oklahoma football protest probably sealed the fate of the offending students. Free speech might be a contested ideal on our campuses, but college football is sacrosanct.[3]

How have universities tried to improve the racial climate on campus?

The first way, not surprisingly, is by hiring more university administrators. New speech codes and affirmative action regulations required institutions to hire new officials to monitor them; so did cultural and support centers for minorities, which have boomed over the past few decades. Likewise, female students demanded and were rewarded with women's centers in the 1970s and 1980s. Then came offices for gays and lesbians, which spiked after the 1998 murder of the gay University of Wyoming student Matthew Shepherd and again after the 2010 suicide of Rutgers student Tyler Clementi, whose roommate surreptitiously recorded him by webcam during a homosexual tryst. Over 180 colleges now have separate LGBT (lesbian-gay-bisexual-transgender) centers; others integrate those services into more broad-gauged multicultural facilities, overseen by yet another set of staffers.

On a growing number of campuses, meanwhile, all of these activities are directed by an entirely new category of

administrator: the chief diversity officer, or CDO. Thirty
CDO offices were created between 2001 and 2006; by 2009,
the National Association of Diversity Officers in Higher
Education listed 107 colleges and universities as "charter
members." Across the American higher-education landscape, to be sure, administrative hiring has exploded; by
2006, indeed, full-time administrators and staffers outnumbered full-time faculty on our campuses. But the growth
has been especially sharp in diversity offices, which—
like speech codes—provide an obvious way for universities to signal that they are addressing problems of race.
In the wake of the November 2015 protests, for example,
Ithaca College pledged to hire its first CDO; Claremont-
McKenna College promised new leadership positions on
"diversity and inclusion"; and Brown University released a
$100 million "Inclusivity Plan," including the creation of a
new center—and, predictably, the hiring of a new dean—
focused on diversity. "[L]iving up to our values means
not just opening Brown's doors to talented people who
have historically been excluded from higher education,"
Brown's president explained, "it means ensuring that these
students, scholars, and staff thrive."

It also means providing a wide range of educational programming, not just support services. By the 1990s, nearly
half of four-year colleges mandated that students take at
least one "multicultural" course as part of their general education requirements. But much of the diversity programming for students was provided directly by administrators,
reflecting the overall emphasis on diversity at our universities as well as the growing power of administrators vis-à-vis
faculty inside of them. It starts with freshman orientation,
where race, gender, and sexuality have become dominant
themes. At the University of Oklahoma, for example, all
freshmen and transfer students must take a five-hour "diversity course." The course had been designed before the

racist fraternity video at Oklahoma surfaced. But publicity surrounding the video certainly accelerated the timetable for implementing the course, which aims to "build empathy for others' perspectives and to develop skills to talk about complicated topics like race," Oklahoma officials explained. Throughout their college years, meanwhile, students are urged—or, occasionally, required—to participate in workshops, seminars, and trainings about diversity and especially about racism; by 1997, one study found, 81 percent of colleges had sponsored events where students discussed experiences of racial bias. Finally, universities also instituted diversity trainings for the faculty. Like so many other recent administrative reforms in higher education, the trainings were borrowed from the corporate world: as early as 1992, two-thirds of major American companies had already conducted diversity trainings for their employees.

As we'll see in Chapter 6, these trainings also reflected the larger psychological and therapeutic impulse of the modern university: the goal was to get each participant to confront her or his subtle and unconscious biases, which was the first step toward changing them. So diversity training sometimes became a kind of "harangue-flagellation ritual," as Elisabeth Lasch-Quinn has written, casting minorities in the role of "angry victims" and whites as "oppressors who need to expiate their guilt." Two-thirds of the demand sheets produced by student protesters last fall called for "diversity training" on campus; and the most frequently identified target for such training was the mostly white professoriate, whose alleged racial blinders made them inattentive to diversity itself. At Dartmouth, for example, students called on the college to "mandate sensitivity training for all faculty" in order to "reduce incidents of racism, sexism, heterosexism, classism, and ableism by faculty towards students." Mindful of professors' often prickly independence, most administrators "recommended" these trainings to faculty but did not require them. The training sessions were mandatory only for fellow staffers, creating an emblematic metaphor for the modern university: administrators talking to administrators. But just like other diversity interventions, they sent a strong message about what the institution valued. So did universities' appointment of "diversity consultants" in faculty hiring searches, another commonplace reform of recent years. As political scientist Benjamin Ginsberg has observed, this practice allowed administrators to insert themselves into what had formerly been a professorial prerogative: the selection of new colleagues. But it probably did little to enhance the actual diversity of the faculty, which won't improve substantially until universities start producing more minority Ph.D.s.[4]

Have universities' efforts to improve the racial climate worked?

It's hard to know. According to Arthur Levine and Diane Dean, who have been surveying college students for several decades, students across the racial spectrum are more satisfied with the racial climate on campus than ever before. Even more, they reported in 2012, racial groups who had formerly disagreed on the subject were starting to converge in their opinions. Students of color were more likely to say that the United States had made important racial gains and less likely to say that minorities should be admitted to the institution even if it means lowering the bar for getting in; meanwhile, an increasing fraction of whites said that their campus needed more diversity and that race-based affirmative action was necessary to achieve it. More students of all races reported that they had friends of a *different* race. Most remarkably, perhaps, fewer students across the racial spectrum agreed that "most American colleges are racist whether they mean to be or not," a founding assumption in many diversity trainings. Of course, the news wasn't all rosy. About half the students said that people of different races "keep to themselves" on campus. And African American students, especially, continued to report flagrant racial insensitivities on the part of white students, especially those who used so-called ghetto slang when talking to blacks. But overall, Levine and Dean concluded, the climate for racial diversity was much improved. And the reason was simple: there was more diversity, period. Just as *Bakke* predicted, the more that students interacted with people different from themselves, the more appreciation of "difference" they would develop.

But it's hardly clear that this changed climate stemmed from anything that universities *did*, in terms of curriculum or programming. Some multicultural course requirements could be satisfied with classes as diffuse as "Food in America" or (at one institution) table tennis; even when the requirement was more narrowly focused on racial and ethnic issues, it was difficult to demonstrate the effect of a single class (or even of several classes) on student perceptions and understanding. The same goes for administrative programming around diversity. Tracking 2,000 students at the richly multiracial University of California–Los Angeles, psychologist Jim Sidanius did find that living with members of different groups increased students' levels of tolerance toward these groups. But the effect was modest, and Sidanius couldn't find *any* effect—positive or negative—from the elaborate (and expensive!) multicultural programming that universities provided. "We, like many intellectuals of the day, expected to find that cultural diversity and the multicultural practices that universities put in place in response to it would have some profound effects on the students," Sidanius and his colleagues wrote in 2008. "We found, however, that students were changed rather little in their ethnic and racial orientations by the college experience." Other scholars reported that some diversity programming might actually increase levels of intergroup prejudice and hostility, suggesting that the best anti prejudice program might be doing nothing at all. Still other researchers found that diversity interventions could alter how students thought about racial differences, but only temporarily; in many cases, students reverted to their former attitudes following a single negative comment or interaction.

And in recent years, as the November 2015 protests illustrated, race relations on campus seem to have taken a turn for the worse. The mostly sunny assessment by Levine and Dean came out of surveys that concluded in 2011. But after that, by most accounts, the racial mood soured. Black students, especially, reported facing hostility from whites "on a daily basis"; they also described widespread feelings of isolation and alienation, echoing the research about race on campus from the 1960s and 1970s. Some observers attributed the shift in attitudes to events beyond the campus, especially the rash of police shootings against unarmed blacks and the subsequent Black Lives Matter movement. Others, ironically, cited university efforts on behalf of diversity itself: the more that an institution hyped its commitment to diversity, minority students said, the more despondent they became about the gap between its rhetoric and reality. That's why protesting students at Hamilton College in 2015 demanded the removal of the college's statement of diversity from its website, which declared: "A student at Hamilton can be grungy, geeky, athletic, gay, black, white, fashionable, artsy, nerdy, preppy, conservative . . . it doesn't really matter. At Hamilton, you can be yourself—and be respected for who you are." But as sociologist Mitchell Stevens admitted, after serving as an admissions officer at the college for a year, the people who ran the institution knew that wasn't true. As much as they might try to deny it, there really *was* a "typical" Hamilton student mold: wealthy, athletic, physically attractive ... and white. And the minority students knew it, too, better than anyone else did. The diversity statement on the website was a noble ideal, to be sure. But it was a far cry from what actually happened at the school, or at most other ones.[5]

4

PROFESSORIAL SPEECH
AND THE FATE OF ACADEMIC
FREEDOM

What is academic freedom?

Here's what it isn't: a license for professors do whatever they want. Consider the case of James Tracy, a tenured associate professor of communications who was fired by Florida Atlantic University in early 2016. Tracy has repeatedly asserted that the 2012 Sandy Hook massacre and other mass shootings were hoaxes; he has also been accused of harassment by a Sandy Hook victim's parents, who said he sent them a certified letter demanding proof that a murdered child was theirs. Significantly, however, the university announced that it was firing Tracy for neglecting his duties rather than for expressing his opinions. It charged that Tracy had failed to submit required paperwork detailing his off-the-job activities, including his blog and radio show. Tracy said he would fight his dismissal, which he called "a matter of free speech." But Florida Atlantic claimed otherwise. It was firing Tracy for "failure to follow university policy," not because of anything he said.

And that also tells you something important about academic freedom in the United States, where we have developed a strong consensus on the value of free speech for our professors. They can't do anything they want, but they can—in theory—*say* anything they want. Over the past century, to be sure, universities have inhibited or muzzled professorial speech in a wide variety of ways. And as we'll see in this chapter, faculty on every side of the political spectrum continue to charge that they are threatened, disciplined, and otherwise constrained in the free exercise of their speech. Indeed, that's precisely what James Tracy is charging: that his university penalized him for expressing his point of view. Only a complete investigation of the case will confirm whether Tracy is correct about Florida Atlantic's motives in dismissing him. But the university's insistence that it was *not* penalizing Tracy for his speech—however outrageous or offensive it was—speaks to the larger point here: whether or not professors are always free to speak their minds, we have a strong normative agreement that they *should* be able to do so.

That's because of their distinctive role in creating knowledge, which requires continuous testing, discussion, and analysis. The process is both idiosyncratic and collective: professors need maximal personal freedom to try out new ideas, but they can't know if they've come up with anything truly new (or useful, or valuable, or visionary) until they have subjected it to a full and free examination by their peers. Hence any threat to their academic freedom threatens the core purpose of the academy itself. "No person of intelligence believes that all of our political problems have been solved, or that the final stage of social evolution has been reached," the American Association of University Professors (AAUP) resolved in 1915, in its first official statement on academic freedom. So the modern university "should be an intellectual experiment station," the AAUP continued, "where new ideas may germinate and where their fruit, though still distasteful to the community as a whole, may be allowed to ripen until finally, perchance, it may become part of the accepted intellectual food of the nation or of the world."[1]

How has academic freedom fared over the past century?

It's a mixed bag. The AAUP's 1915 statement came near the end of the Progressive Era, when several professors lost their jobs for advocating union rights, public ownership of utilities, and other reforms that rubbed universities' plutocratic trustees the wrong way. At Stanford, for example, founder Leland Stanford's widow explained that one fired professor "plays into the hands of the lowest and vilest elements of socialism." Writing in 1915, philosopher John Dewey—one of America's most eminent intellectuals, and a key force behind the AAUP statement—predicted that these kinds of dismissals would soon disappear. But shortly thereafter, he was forced to admit that he had been wrong. At least 20 professors lost their jobs for questioning or denouncing America's entry into World War I, when the AAUP quickly backtracked on its nascent commitment to academic freedom: during the war, the AAUP resolved, professors should avoid saying anything that encouraged opposition to it. "What had been tolerated before becomes intolerable now," declared President Nicholas Murray Butler of Columbia University, where the prominent historian and author Charles Beard resigned in protest. But most American professors didn't appear to find anything wrong with the new strictures. And most of the others bit their tongues to save their skins.

The next great challenge to academic freedom came after the next world war, in the early 1950s. But the stage was set a few years earlier, with the 1940 passage of the Smith Act barring Americans from advocating the violent overthrow of their government or from joining organizations (read: the Communist Party) that supported the same. The AAUP released yet another statement on academic freedom in the wake of the Smith Act, confirming professors' speech rights but warning them to avoid discussion of "controversial matter" that was not related to their topics of research or instruction. From here on in, the AAUP's 1940 statement confirmed, professors' most serious challenges would come not from trustees or administrators inside the university but from politicians and other critics outside of it. Academic freedom would be the sentinel, in theory, guarding the college gates against the rabble hordes beyond them.

Yet faced with its biggest test, academic freedom again fell short. The fire-breathing Wisconsin senator Joseph McCarthy and his fellow Red-hunters took particular aim at the university in the early 1950s, suspecting it of harboring Communists and their fellow travelers; indeed, nearly one-fifth of the witnesses called before congressional and state investigating committees during the McCarthy era were professors or graduate students. Over 100 professors lost their jobs or were denied tenure because of their actual or assumed political leanings, and with only one exception, every accused professor who did *not* have tenure was fired. Surveying American faculty after the McCarthyite attacks cooled, sociologist Paul Lazarsfeld counted 990 separate incidents in which professors were charged with Communist Party membership or sympathies. More scholars came to their colleagues' defense than during World War I. But many others stayed quiet or actively supported the quest to purge Communists from the university. Some defenders said that so-called Red professors were a threat to national security; others argued that their supposedly slavish devotion to communism should disqualify them from the academy, which was premised upon, yes, the free exchange of ideas. Ironically, then, the same ideal that undergirded academic freedom—full and unbridled discussion—was invoked to undo it.

In a further irony, academic freedom would soon receive a big boost from the same institution that had done so much to undermine it: the federal government. The

Supreme Court issued a ringing affirmation of academic freedom in *Sweezy v. New Hampshire* (1957), which upheld a professor who had refused to reply to questions about his political background. "Scholarship cannot flourish in an atmosphere of suspicion and distrust," the Court proclaimed, echoing the AAUP's 1915 statement. "Teachers and students must always remain free to inquire, to study and to evaluate, to gain new maturity and understanding; otherwise our civilization will stagnate and die." A decade later, in *Keyshian v. Board of Regents* (1967), the Court struck down a required New York loyalty oath for teachers and professors. This time it was even more emphatic, warning against a "pall of orthodoxy" in American schools and universities. "The classroom is peculiarly the 'marketplace of ideas,'" the *Keyshian* decision declared. "The Nation's future depends upon leaders trained through wide exposure to that robust exchange of ideas which discovers truth 'out of a multitude of tongues, [rather] than through any kind of authoritative selection.'" A decade after that, in *Regents of the University of California v. Bakke* (1978), the Court would quote the same words in upholding affirmative action. By widening the racial diversity of the university, *Bakke* argued, affirmative action would enhance *Keyshian's* "multitude of tongues."[2]

Did academic freedom come under fire after the 9/11 attacks?

Plenty of professors certainly thought so. Five years after the September 11, 2001, attacks on the World Trade Center and the Pentagon, the editor of a book on academic freedom declared flatly that it was "facing its most serious threat since the McCarthy era." Predictably, given the source of the 9/11 attacks and the wars that they unleashed, scholars of the Middle East often faced the most serious threat of all.

In certain quarters, indeed, anyone who tried to analyze the attacks in historical or political context was denounced as an apologist for them. After several scholars held a post-9/11 teach-in at the City University of New York (CUNY), the *New York Post* skewered the event as a "peacefest" staged by "blind, stupid, or intellectually dishonest" professors who confused the "divisive war in Vietnam" with the "coming war against terrorism that's uniting Americans." Commenting on the teach-in, CUNY's own chancellor condemned professors "who seek to justify or make lame excuses for the attacks."

Two months after 9/11, the right-leaning American Council of Trustees and Alumni (ACTA) released a report that upped the ante: in addition to apologizing for America's enemies, the ACTA charged, the university hadn't instilled students with sufficient patriotism to stand up to them. The title of its report spoke volumes: "Defending Civilization: How Our Universities Are Failing America and What Can Be Done About It." It included 117 recent remarks by faculty, students, and staff that illustrated the university's supposedly inadequate reaction to the 9/11 tragedy, including "Ignorance breeds hate" and "There needs to be an understanding of why this kind of suicidal violence could be undertaken against our country." Under fire for directly identifying the sources of these comments, the ACTA eventually removed their names from its website. But their quotations (as well as their institutional affiliations) remained, highlighting the allegedly weak-kneed response of the academy to the deadliest attack on American soil since Pearl Harbor.

Other critics blasted the entire field of Middle East Studies, which they said was biased toward Arabs, Palestinians, and Muslims and against Israel, the United States, and Jews. The U.S. House of Representatives twice passed a bill that would have barred grants to federally funded centers for Middle East Studies unless the grants were approved by a set of political appointees, including two representatives of national security agencies; although the bill died in the Senate both times, it reflected the larger animus against the field outside of the university. The campaign was spearheaded by Daniel Pipes, founder and editor of the *Campus Watch* website, which lobbed a constant set of volleys at Middle East Studies professors, courses, and publications. A leading target was Columbia's department of Middle East and Asian Languages and Cultures (MEALAC), where a junior professor named Joseph Massad was charged with shouting down students who did not share his perspective. "If you're going to deny the atrocities being committed against Palestinians, then you can get out of my classroom!" Massad allegedly yelled. He denied the charge, as did his teaching assistant, but it reappeared in a film documentary—*Columbia Unbecoming*—produced by pro-Israel critics of Massad and other members of his department. A university grievance committee cleared the department of bias and intimidation charges in 2005, although it did confirm that two witnesses had corroborated the shouting incident involving Massad. He was awarded tenure shortly after that, over the objections of 14 colleagues who urged Columbia to reconsider its decision.

Other professors weren't so fortunate, including several who were penalized for in-class comments in the wake of 9/11. The first casualty was Richard Berthold, a senior historian at the University of New Mexico, who greeted 100 new freshmen in his Western Civilization class on September 11, 2001, by announcing, "Anybody who blows up the Pentagon gets my vote." Picked up by the national news media, Berthold's remark elicited death threats over email and calls for his dismissal on talk radio and in the state legislature. He later apologized, calling his words "an exercise in incredible callousness," but the damage was done; the university removed him from the Western Civ class, and he retired the following year. At Colorado State University, likewise, a part-time instructor was removed from his classroom after a student whose husband was serving in the Iraq War took offense at the instructor's claim that President George W. Bush was "sending boys and girls out to die for no goddam reason." He received death threats as well, prompting the instructor to change his phone number and obtain a firearm. And in at least one case, a university employee was punished for comments made outside of class. The University of California–Los Angeles suspended a librarian for a week for sending out a group email asserting that American taxpayers "fund and arm an apartheid state called Israel" and asking, "So, who are the 'terrorists' anyway?"[3]

Did professors' opinions after 9/11 cost them their jobs?

Perhaps so, in a very small number of cases. The most controversial one involved University of Colorado ethnic studies professor Ward Churchill, who was fired after publishing an essay referring to 9/11 victims as "little Eichmanns." As in the case of James Tracy, the fired Florida Atlantic professor who said Sandy Hook was a hoax, Colorado officials insisted that their decision had nothing to do with Churchill's incendiary remark; indeed, a university investigatory committee explicitly acknowledged that his comment was protected speech under the First Amendment, and that Churchill could not be dismissed for it. But the university fired him anyway after a second committee ruled that he had plagiarized parts of his research and had also published statements lacking scholarly evidence, including a much-repeated tale that the U.S. Army had deliberately provided smallpox-infected blankets to

Native Americans in North Dakota. A self-described pro-vocateur who never earned a Ph.D., Churchill certainly failed to follow scholarly norms of attribution and verification. But just as surely, as a jury ruled in a lawsuit Churchill filed, the university would never have expended so much energy in reviewing his scholarship if he hadn't published his 9/11 essay.

At DePaul University, meanwhile, the political scientist and longtime Israel critic Norman Finkelstein was denied tenure despite strong votes of support from his department and a college-wide faculty panel. But after a firestorm of protest from outside critics, including the media-savvy Harvard law professor Alan Dershowitz, DePaul's board of tenure and promotion turned Finkelstein down. Once again, school officials insisted that his opinions were not at issue; he was rejected instead for his lack of "collegiality," a catch-all phrase that surely describes countless other professors as well. If not for 9/11 and the heated political atmosphere that followed it, it's hard to believe that Finkelstein's prickly personality would have led DePaul to deny him tenure.

Several professors of Middle Eastern descent also faced challenges in the post-9/11 years, adding the always-thorny question of race to the larger deliberations over academic freedom. The University of South Florida fired Kuwaiti-born computer engineering professor Sami Amin Al-Arian after the federal government accused him of giving material support to a Palestinian terrorist organization; acquitted of the most serious charge, Al-Arian eventually pleaded guilty to a lesser one and was finally deported in 2015. Significantly, however, the university didn't accuse Al-Arian of academic misconduct or convene a committee to investigate the same. It simply ruled that Al-Arian's presence would cause "academic disruption" and threaten campus security, which essentially convicted him before the government did.

Most recently, the University of Illinois rescinded a job offer to Palestinian American literature scholar Steven Salaita after his anti-Israel tweets on social media caught the eye of university officials. One tweet said that defenders of Israel are either "hopelessly brainwashed" or "awful human beings"; another asked whether anyone would be surprised if Israeli Prime Minister Benjamin Netanyahu appeared on television wearing "a necklace made from the teeth of Palestinian children." Borrowing language from the debate over hate speech, the university's chancellor said that Salaita's offer was withdrawn because he used "disrespectful words" that "demean and abuse" others. But the university eventually paid Salaita $600,000 plus legal fees to settle a lawsuit he filed; to Salaita, that sent "a strong message to those who would silence Palestine activists and limit speech on campus," as he wrote on his Facebook page.

At the same time, some pro-Israel and Jewish professors say that *their* academic freedom has been under attack since 9/11. They point especially to the Boycott, Divestment and Sanctions (BDS) movement on campuses, which started shortly after the September 11 attacks and has picked up steam in recent years. Some of these campaigns call on universities to divest from companies doing business in Israel; others assert that professors and students should refrain from participating in Israeli conferences, study tours, and scholarly partnerships. Over 1,000 professors on more than 300 American campuses have endorsed an academic boycott of Israel, which has also been approved by the American Studies Association, the National Women's Studies Association, and several smaller scholarly organizations. Jewish professors and students have charged that BDS supporters harass them during so-called Israeli Apartheid Week, when protesters dressed as Israeli soldiers—and carrying fake guns—establish mock military checkpoints on campus. Most of all, though, critics of the BDS movement claim that the boycott itself violates academic freedom by inhibiting a full and free exchange of ideas. Here they can claim the support of the AAUP, which has likened the boycott to loyalty oaths and other "ideological litmus tests" that limited academic freedom in the past. To be sure, the AAUP recently resolved, individual faculty members retain the right to associate—or not—with whomever they choose. But "when such noncooperation takes the form of a systematic academic boycott," the AAUP argued, "it threatens the principles of free expression and communication on which we collectively depend."[4]

Is there a "New McCarthyism" on American campuses?

That's an easy one: no. Middle East Studies professors and BDS opponents have both sought to delegitimize their opponents by charging them with establishing a latter-day McCarthyism. But they actually discredit themselves by this wild claim, which exaggerates the dangers of the present and minimizes the abuses of the past. Yes, as we saw in Chapter 1, significant fractions of professors as well as students report that they censor their own opinions to guard against ridicule or harm. Whatever the threats to academic freedom on campuses today, however, they cannot—and should not—be compared to the catastrophe of the McCarthy era, when dozens of professors saw their careers destroyed simply because of their assumed political predilections. Indeed, our bipartisan penchant for flinging "the M word"—as a term of disapproval, of course—speaks to the vastly stronger norms of academic freedom today. It wasn't so long ago that conservatives like William F. Buckley were questioning whether professors should have academic freedom at all: in his first book,

God and Man at Yale (subtitle: *The Superstitions of Academic Freedom*), Buckley argued that universities should teach the allegedly timeless truths of Christianity and capitalism instead of encouraging professors to undermine these truths in their scholarship and teaching. Buckley's next book (*McCarthy and His Enemies*, 1954) was a full-throated defense of the Wisconsin senator and his anti-Communist purge; to Buckley and his co-author L. Brent Bozell, who was also Buckley's brother-in-law, McCarthyism was "a movement around which men of good will and stern morality can close ranks." Today, by contrast, virtually everyone at the academy agrees that McCarthyism was a disaster for academic life. Calling your enemy a McCarthyite is almost always unwarranted, but our shared revulsion at the term also reveals how far we have come from McCarthyism itself.

So does the widespread support for people whose academic freedom has come under fire. In earlier eras, as we've seen, many professors sat on their hands when colleagues were penalized or dismissed on account of their politics. Today, by contrast, the profession has rallied behind virtually every faculty member whose public statements have placed her or him in peril. The AAUP flew an entire team to Florida to support Sami Amin Al-Arian, demanding that his institution conduct a full hearing about its decision to pre emptively dismiss him. It also threw its full weight behind Norman Finkelstein, calling off its campaign only after he reached a monetary settlement with DePaul. Most remarkably, perhaps, the AAUP has even defended the academic freedom of the Sandy Hook "truther" James Tracy. No matter how outrageous Tracy's remarks, the AAUP has asserted, his university simply cannot and must not penalize him for them. "Professor Tracy may indeed have posted highly controversial statements on his website," the AAUP declared in 2013, when Tracy first came under fire, "but it is such speech, in particular, that requires the protection of academic freedom."

But the profession has been somewhat slower to defend faculty charged with making inappropriate sexual statements rather than controversial "political" ones. As we'll see in the next chapter, universities have recently altered their sexual assault policies in response to federal warnings that they could be in violation of anti discrimination and harassment laws. But these same policies have also been used to threaten or penalize professors whose speech—not behavior—allegedly contributed to a hostile atmosphere in campus. The most egregious example involved Northwestern University communications professor Laura Kipnis, who published an article in 2015 condemning the excessive policing of sexual conduct and speech on campus; as if to prove her right, students marched on the president's office to demand a "swift, official condemnation" of her. Northwestern officials refused, citing Kipnis's academic freedom, but other institutions have routinely sanctioned their own faculty in similar situations. At the University of Denver, a tenured professor was found guilty of sexual harassment and suspended for teaching about sexual themes in his class about the war on drugs; officials especially objected to a course unit entitled "Drugs and Sin in American Life: From Masturbation and Prostitution to Alcohol and Drugs." Most recently—and most alarmingly—a tenured professor at Louisiana State University was fired for making sexual comments in class. She reportedly described someone exhibiting cowardly behavior as "being a pussy," and she also joked that sex got worse as relationships got longer. The professor said she used these terms to get students' attention, but the university said she was "creating a hostile learning environment." Under federal law, then, it was the school's duty to sanction her.

To be sure, academic freedom does not and should not protect professors who make sexual advances to students or make truly harassing and threatening remarks to them. But when a professor at San Bernardino College can be punished for assigning an essay asking students to define "pornography"—not to defend it, mind you, simply to *define* it—then we have a problem for academic freedom. A recent external audit of Occidental College found that professors and students were reluctant to comment about the sexual assault controversy on campus for fear of "ostracism and retaliation" from either school administrators or student activists. Anyone who raised doubts about the veracity of a particular assault charge—or about the college's process for adjudicating it—risked being accused of "blaming the victim"; by the same token, anything that an alleged victim said or did was seen as above reproach. "Colleges and universities ought to be places in which one can have difficult discussions," the Occidental president said, citing the free-and-full exchange ideal at the heart of academic freedom. "Instead we've succumbed to the same kind of polarized atmosphere that we see on the national stage."

Whatever the issue under discussion, finally, the most vulnerable professors are those in America's expanding army of so-called adjunct or contingent faculty. As we've seen, full-time professors have extraordinary leeway in what they can say; their speech is almost always "protected," even when it's offensive or just flat-out false. But these protections typically don't apply to the part-time faculty, who now make up more than two-thirds of the people who teach at American colleges and universities. That's why "The Phantom Professor"—an adjunct instructor at Southern Methodist University—kept her identity hidden while blogging about student drug use and other problems on the campus; when the university discovered her real name she was fired, just as she had feared. In Virginia, an adjunct instructor who told his class that the 2007 massacre at Virginia State University had been overhyped by the national media—because so many victims were white women—was dismissed the very next day. An Iowa adjunct was fired for calling the biblical story of Adam and Eve a "myth," and another part-timer wasn't renewed by his university after students complained that he had assigned them "offensive" course readings, including one by Mark Twain. It's impossible to imagine these fates befalling full-time professors, who have the powerful bulwark of academic freedom behind them. And as many of our high-profile academic freedom cases illustrate—think Laura Kipnis or Joseph Massad—the academic guild does a pretty good job protecting people with full-time positions. But the rest of the profession—indeed, the *majority* of the profession—is left to fend for itself. Most of our adjunct faculty simply don't have real academic freedom, which might be the biggest academic freedom scandal of all.[5]

5

STUDENT BODIES

POLICING SEX ON COLLEGE CAMPUSES

What is in loco parentis?

In loco parentis means, literally, "in place of a parent." And for most of our history, universities acted as one. They made all of the the rules governing student life, in the dormitory and classroom and everywhere else. And the colleges could discipline students who ran afoul of them, just like Mom and Dad did when the kids were at home. Students were penalized for smoking, drinking, failing to attend chapel, and for protesting these restrictions or the long list of other ones. The rules were especially rigid for women, who were typically barred from entertaining men in their rooms; when men were allowed, a whole other set of codes mandated that doors remain ajar and the people inside keep their legs on the floor. Under these "parietal rules," as they became known, women were also required to sign out of their dorms in the evenings—indicating where they were going, and with whom—and to maintain a curfew, which sometimes varied by the night of the week, the student's year in college, or even by her grade point average. By 1962, the 15-page student handbook at the University Michigan devoted nine of those pages to rules for women.

That reflected an obvious and explicit double standard surrounding sex, which was tacitly accepted for college men but strictly taboo for college women. As early as the 1920s, surveys of male undergraduates showed that about one-third of them had engaged in sexual intercourse. But most of them did so with a prostitute or "charity girl," a working-class woman who traded sex for a night on the town. Men distinguished these so-called pickups from dates, the college women who escorted them to dances and other social events—and who were supposed to remain chaste until marriage. But they were also expected to engage in "petting"—the era's catch all term for sexual behavior that fell short of intercourse—which would keep your date interested but your "reputation" intact. Just how far you should go was a subject of intense deliberation, as one older observer at a conference of 800 college women in 1925 confirmed. "The girls did not advise younger class-men not to pet—they merely advised them to be moderate about it," she wrote, "Learn temperance in petting, not abstinence."

The double standard endured into the 1950s, when college men began to press student "coeds"—not just working-class girlfriends—for sex. "The boy demonstrated his desirability by demanding more and more erotic satisfaction," the prominent anthropologist Margaret Mead wrote, "while the girl demonstrated her sureness of her own popularity by refusing his request." Actually, as Alfred T. Kinsey's famous surveys confirmed, rising numbers of young women as well as young men were having sex. At colleges, they developed elaborate ruses to circumvent parietal rules. Some of them climbed into dorm rooms through windows; others signed out to the library, then went to motels instead. Or they simply took to their cars, if they owned one, leading some colleges to set new rules on the use of automobiles as well. "We wouldn't care if cars had no wheels, just so long as they had doors," quipped one Oberlin student, denouncing the college's auto restrictions. Others undermined parietal rules by performing impish satires of them: to mock the common requirement that dorm doors stay open by the length of a book, for example, women placed a matchbook in their doors when hosting a man.[1]

What happened to in loco parentis?

In a word, the Sixties happened. Instead of evading or criticizing specific *in loco parentis* rules, students in the 1960s asked why colleges should get to act as parents in the first place. Their first target were restrictions on organized protests, which themselves triggered the first great burst of protest in Cal-Berkeley's Free Speech Movement of 1964. But the Free Speech Movement was never just about free speech; it was about freedom from all of the university's invidious and arbitrary rules, ranging from arcane course requirements to restrictions on sex. The outbreak of the Vietnam War further fanned campus resistance to dorm sign-outs, four-legs-on-the floor codes, and all the rest: if students were adult enough to fight and die in Southeast Asia, they argued, surely they should be allowed to conduct their personal lives as adults as well.

The question came to a head in 1968, when the *New York Times* ran a piece about an unnamed pair of students— she at Barnard, he at Columbia—who were living together in an off-campus apartment. They were soon identified as Linda LeClair and Peter Behr, who became the somewhat accidental vanguard in the revolution against *in loco parentis*. Speaking before hundreds at a Barnard public hearing, LeClair argued that *in loco parentis* discriminated against women because men weren't subject to the same constraints. Barnard soon eliminated its parietal rules, over the objections of alumni and angry readers in the national press; to one appalled critic, Barnard's surrender to student whims confirmed that "a bunch of glorified whores go to eastern colleges." He was right about one thing: *in loco parentis* was disappearing, almost everywhere you looked. To be sure, religious colleges retained a range of parietal rules; and into the present, according to a recent study of 1,300 institutions, 43 secular colleges continue to prohibit opposite-sex overnight guests in their residence halls. But the vast majority of American universities did away with their parietal rules by the late-1970s. Simply put, the rules had lost their legitimacy among the younger generation.

They also lost their legal sanction, as judicial doctrine on the subject shifted. Going back nearly a century, courts had given universities free rein in exercising *in loco parentis*; the founding case was *Gott v. Berea College* (1913), where the Kentucky Supreme Court—upholding a rule that barred students from patronizing a local restaurant—confirmed that colleges can "make any rule or regulation for the government or betterment of their pupils that a parent could for the same purpose." After that, a Michigan court upheld the expulsion of a student for smoking, and a court in New York allowed Syracuse University to dismiss a female student for conduct "unbecoming a typical Syracuse girl. " But in 1961, a federal court in Alabama overturned the expulsion of students from a historically black college who had participated in a sit-in against segregation. That triggered an avalanche of decisions against *in loco parentis*, which was now held to violate students' due-process rights under the 14th Amendment. The death knell was probably sounded with the ratification of the 26th Amendment in 1971, which lowered the voting age to 18. Just as students were old enough to serve in a war, they were now old enough to cast a ballot. So it seemed increasingly absurd for colleges to say that they were too young to have sex.[2]

What happened to sex at college after in loco parentis *ended?*

Here's what *didn't* happen: a nonstop orgy of casual or anonymous sex. That's the impression you might get from reading some accounts in the national media. But surveys of students themselves tell a different story. About 40 percent of students report that they are virgins or that they have only had sex once, while 70 percent report having only one sexual partner over the past year. At the same time, about 70 percent of students also report "hooking up" with an acquaintance—that is, someone who is not a romantic partner—during college; men report an average of ten hookups by senior year, and women report an average of seven. But "hookup" is a notoriously imprecise word, and it often doesn't mean what scandalous media exposes assume. Only 40 percent of students say that their most recent hookup included intercourse; the rest involved oral sex and a wide range of other behaviors, many of which would be fully recognizable to the "petting" generations of yesteryear.

What's truly new is the much more explicit public discussion of sex, especially in the student press. Editors at Cal-Berkeley's *Daily Californian* pioneered the nation's first regular college sex column in 1996, in the wake of student protests against the paper about a much more controversial topic: race. After the *Daily Cal* ran an editorial backing Proposition 209, the state ballot measure that barred race-based affirmative action in university admissions, thieves stole the paper's entire press run of 2,300 copies (the largest newspaper theft in college history) and protesters rushed into its offices, ripping up newspapers and tossing them off the balcony. A week later, an editor at the paper proposed a sex column as a kind of olive branch. "We knew those people who were storming our halls wouldn't be up in arms about sex," he recalled. "There are certain issues people would be enraged about, and sex just wasn't one of them." It also promised to revive the dismal economic fortunes of the independently published paper, which had dwindled to a twice-a-week schedule and had even considered bankruptcy. Hundreds of college publications soon started their own sex columns, which seemed to make the student press relevant again. At Ohio State University, the college paper got much more feedback about its sex column than it did about America's 2003 invasion of Iraq. "Forget the fighting," a former editor quipped. "Students want to talk about sex."

Meanwhile, some of their elders want to muzzle them. Like any story involving students and sex, the new college columns made a big splash in the national media. Then came the calls for censorship, which were every bit as predictable. After the paper at Northern Arizona University ran a February column called, "On Valentine's Day, nothing says 'I love you' like oral sex," state legislators proposed a ban on public funding for student newspapers at Arizona's three public universities; apparently, the lawmakers didn't realize that all of the papers were independently funded. Administrators at several other colleges around the country condemned sex columns and occasionally tried to prevent papers from publishing them, which students decried as an attack on their constitutional freedoms. As the Cal-Berkeley episode illustrates, students have sometimes questioned newspapers' right to discuss questions of race. When it came to sex, however, everyone became a warrior for free speech. "While banning a sex column from a student newspaper may seem like a minor issue," a Michigan student editor wrote in 2009, "any infringement upon a student newspaper's right to print the content it deems relevant to students violates not only the First Amendment but also the very foundations of ethical journalism." The title of his column made the point even more explicitly: "Free speech is sexy."

On campus and off, however, some readers continued to complain that student sex-talk was simply *too* explicit. Even college staffers who prided themselves on their liberal instincts were embarrassed by "detailed descriptions of vaginas and penises and positions and tactics" in the student press, as one administrator told Arthur Levine and Diane Dean. "I'm not a prude, so young people screw," he continued. "That's what they have always done and always will do. We did. But it is different now and the explicit[ness] of it. . . . We're sixties baby boomers, but whoa we can't do that." Other observers have been struck by the seemingly unromantic quality of student discourse on sex: there's lots of chatter abut "dormcest," booty calls, and hookups but little about dating, romance, or lovemaking. Trying to keep up with the times while protecting student health, colleges have sponsored extensive safe-sex campaigns that often sport a humorous touch: one school hosts "condom bingo" in the cafeteria (with condoms used as board markers), while another sponsors "happy hump day" each Wednesday, when condoms are distributed on the steps of the library. Such efforts have raised occasional hackles among more conservatively oriented students, who have picketed safe-sex events with "Reasons to Wait" flyers. And as critics correctly note, it's hardly clear that these campaigns are having the desired effect on student behavior. Despite the widespread availability of condoms on campus, nearly 40 percent of the students surveyed by Levine and Dean said they never, rarely, or only sometimes use one during intercourse.[3]

When did sexual assault on campus become a problem?

Sexual assault has been around campus for as long as sex has. A little-noticed 1957 study found that one-fifth of college women had been victims of forceful attempted intercourse and that 6 percent of their dates had used "menacing threats or coercive infliction of physical pain" to obtain sex. But campus sexual assault didn't become a heavily discussed public issue until the 1980s, when a survey financed by the Ms. Foundation reported that one in four women at college had been the victim of rape or attempted rape. The Ms. study also found that 90 percent of the victims knew their attacker, belying the common myth of sexual assault as a crime committed by strangers; perhaps most troublingly, however, three-quarters of these victims did not identify their experience as rape. By the 1990s, more and more women started to do so—and in a very public fashion. Thirty male students at Brown were listed by name on the walls of a women's bathroom as perpetrators of "date rape," which helped bring that term into the college *lingua franca*. To focus attention on the issue, meanwhile, art students at the University of Maryland selected 50 men at random from the campus directory and created posters including their names and the caption, "Potential Rapists." Other critics found a new set of villains in college administrators, who were accused of downplaying or ignoring sexual assault in order to protect their institutions' prestige and reputation. The talk-show impresario Larry King hosted several student date-rape victims in the early 1990s, who all said that their colleges knew about the problem but swept it under the rug.

Fearing student lawsuits as well as adverse publicity, universities developed freshman orientation units on sexual violence and other awareness-raising activities for the wider college community. But that didn't assuage their critics, who demanded more prompt investigation of campus sexual assault and more severe punishment for those found guilty of it. Columbia led the way in 2000 by establishing a new administrative post—"coordinator of sexual misconduct and education"—to oversee both prevention and adjudication of sexual assault; it also announced that all charges would be investigated by a panel composed of "specially trained" staffers and students. But the process met immediate criticism from law school professors at Columbia and from the wider civil liberties community in New York, because accused students could neither attend their hearings nor confront their accusers. "It is remarkable that students are pushing for a procedure that allows students to be expelled after what is literally a Star Chamber proceeding," declared law professor Gerard Lynch. Prefiguring recent feminist critiques of campus sexual-assault policies, a letter from Feminists for Free Expression (whose board included Betty Friedan and Erica Jong) charged that the new policy "infantilized students" by denying "the accountability of the accuser." Women, they said, were strong enough to speak freely for themselves without denying or diminishing the freedoms of others.

The next big campus sexual-assault controversy came in 2006, when three white lacrosse players at Duke were falsely accused of raping an African American stripper whom they had hired to perform at their off-campus house. Eighty-eight faculty members signed a statement condemning the students before they were cleared of the charges, which also led to the resignation and disbarment of a local prosecutor for making deceptive statements in the case. The accused students were hardly paragons of virtue: after quarreling with the alleged victim and a second stripper about the fee for their services, one white student yelled, "Tell your grandfather I said thanks for my cotton shirt." The toxic stew of race (and racism) in the case surely made onlookers more likely to rush to judgment against the students; so did the involvement of varsity athletes, who are more likely than other college men to engage in sexual violence and to agree with "rape-supportive statements" such as "about half of women who report rapes to the police are lying." In the Duke case, as it turned out, the reporting woman really *was* lying. But the case doesn't seem to have made colleges warier of falsely charging students of sexual assault. Instead, they continued to act on the premise that "it is more important to discover the truth than to protect the rights of the accused at any cost," as journalist Jon Krakauer wrote recently in his close study of rape in one college town.[4]

What is Title IX?

Colleges' quest to identify and punish sexual assault—and, critics said, their neglect of the rights of the accused—gained steam in 2011, when federal authorities instructed them to use a "preponderance of evidence" standard. That meant institutions should find people guilty if it was more likely than not that they committed sexual assault, not if their guilt was (as in the criminal justice system) beyond reasonable doubt. Here federal officials cited Title IX of the Education Amendments of 1972, which outlawed sex discrimination in educational institutions receiving federal assistance. Up to that point, Title IX was invoked mainly in efforts to correct gender imbalances in college sports. (And it worked: between 1971 and 2012, the percentage of women among American college athletes nearly tripled, from 15 to 43 percent.) Now federal officials were applying it to sexual assault, warning that colleges failing to comply with the new guidelines would be in violation of Title IX and could lose federal funds. Schools were advised not just to lower the burden of evidence but also to allow accusers to appeal nonguilty verdicts, which raised the specter of double jeopardy for the accused. Students facing sexual assault charges could attend their hearings and also bring a lawyer, but they weren't allowed to speak with the lawyer during the proceeding. And federal authorities "strongly" discouraged institutions from allowing the accused to cross-examine his accuser or other witnesses; three years later, authorities warned that schools allowing cross-examination could be charged with perpetuating a "hostile environment," which is illegal under Title IX.

The new federal parameters unleashed a spate of so-called "Title IX complaints," spurred by campus activist groups with names like Know Your IX and Title IX Action Network. In 2014, the Department of Education's Office for Civil Rights released the names of 55 colleges under investigation for violating federal law in their handling of sexual-assault cases, including elite private schools like Harvard, Princeton, and Dartmouth and well-known public ones such as Indiana University, the University of Michigan, and Ohio State University. By the following year the list had swelled to 124 schools, ranging from Full Sail University in Florida—the first for-profit college to come under investigation—to Stanford, Cornell, and the University of Rochester. Columbia was added to the list, too, gaining national notoriety when one student resolved to carry her mattress with her everywhere on campus (including to her graduation ceremony) until her alleged rapist was expelled. Eager to avoid yet more negative press, universities responded by creating campus task forces and numerous other administrative initiatives around the issue. By 2015, some college presidents reported that they were spending fully half of their time on sexual-assault matters alone.

Colleges also established revised standards of "affirmative consent," which required both partners in every encounter to give explicit approval for each new level of sexual activity. Here, too, the colleges were following the lead of the federal government. On NotAlone.gov, the official federal website regarding Title IX, institutions were urged to add three features to their definitions of consent: it can be withdrawn at any time, past consent doesn't imply consent in the future, and it can't be granted by someone who is incapacitated. It wasn't enough to say that "no means no," that is, everyone has a right to reject any sexual act or advance. The new mantra was "yes means yes": each and every act must be affirmatively approved by both parties. Back in the 1990s, when Antioch College established a similar rule, it became a national laughingstock: *Saturday Night Live* produced a skit mocking Antioch's suggested line of intimate questioning (boy to girl: "Is *this* cool?"), while critics on the left as well as the right dismissed the code as political correctness gone wild. "With its overtones of enforcing tolerance and prescribing behaviour it was perhaps inevitable that PC should lead to such absurdities as the Antioch College code," wrote one feminist critic from England, "which insisted on verbal agreement before any and every stage of sexual courtship." Two decades later, that's become the accepted best practice in higher education. By 2016, 1,500 institutions—and two state educational systems, in California and New York—had adopted affirmative-consent standards.

But there would always be ambiguity about sexual consent, no matter how hard the colleges worked to define it. And things got even more confusing when you factored in alcohol, which is involved for both men and women in 80 percent of college sexual assaults. We can all agree—as per the federal guidelines—that someone who is "incapacitated" by liquor can't consent to sex. But how much alcohol renders you incapacitated? And what if both parties are? At Occidental College, for example, a female student filed a complaint against a male student after a drunken sexual encounter that neither could remember the next morning; so it would seem that both were violating the college sexual-assault policy, which bars students from having sex with anyone who is incapacitated by drugs or alcohol. But only the male party was found guilty of sexual assault, which led to his expulsion. He then filed a suit against Occidental, alleging that the school applied its consent rules unfairly against him because of his gender. A similar case also led to litigation against Duke, where a dean openly confirmed the double standard. If both parties are drunk, she testified in the lawsuit, "it is the responsibility in the case of the male to gain consent before proceeding with sex."[5]

Are the rights of the accused sufficiently protected?

It all depends on whom you ask, of course. Many students continue to complain that their universities don't do enough to investigate and prosecute sexual assault; they also express deep skepticism (often shading into cynicism) about administrative leaders, whom they see as more invested in burnishing their own reputations than in protecting students from rape. Especially in the legal community, however, some critics worry that the new guidelines run roughshod over the rights of the accused. In 2014, 28 professors at Harvard Law School signed a letter arguing that the university's sexual-assault procedures "lack the most basic elements of fairness and due process." Another group of Harvard Law professors signed a second statement in 2015 critiquing the documentary film *The Hunting Ground*, which told the stories of four women who said they were sexually assaulted on campus. One of them had been a student at Harvard Law, which investigated her case at length and exonerated her alleged assailant (who was also cleared by a criminal court). But none of that information appeared in the film, which simply ignored his side of the story. "It is a near-religious teaching among many people today that if you are against sexual assault, then you must always believe individuals who say they have been assaulted," wrote one Harvard professor. To be sure, the professor added, America's excruciating history of sexual coercion was studded with "bias against victims." But she warned against inverting that bias with an equally flawed one, which holds that "an accuser must always and unthinkingly be fully believed."

That mistake was on vivid and tragic display in 2014, with the publication of a splashy 9,000-word cover story in *Rolling Stone* magazine about an alleged gang rape at a University of Virginia fraternity (UVA) two years earlier. Under pressure from student groups and other parts of the community, the university president suspended all campus Greek organizations—not just the one where the alleged rape took place—until the following semester. Within a few short weeks, however, the accuser's story began to unravel. Newspaper reporters discovered multiple holes and contradictions in her account; even more, they found out that *Rolling Stone* had never attempted to corroborate it by contacting her alleged assailants. The magazine eventually retracted the story, which had also claimed that the dean who headed UVA's sexual misconduct board had tried to suppress the woman's report of rape in order to protect the university. In fact, the dean arranged a meeting for the alleged victim with the local police, connected her to sexual-assault support groups, and asked her to encourage other victims of assault at the fraternity in question to come forward so the university could build a case against it. The dean eventually sued *Rolling Stone*, as did three former members of the fraternity. The *Rolling Stone* story fit snugly into the generic narrative of campus sexual assault, right down to the frat-boy rapists and the foot-dragging administrator, which surely explains why so many people believed it. But this time it wasn't true.

It's hard to know how many other people have been falsely accused of sexual assault on American campuses. The higher-education insurance group United Educators paid 262 claims to students in college sexual-assault cases between 2006 and 2010, at a total cost to the group of $36 million; nearly three-quarters of the payouts went to accused perpetrators rather than to victims of assault. And since the federal government's initial Title IX directive in 2011, over 20 lawsuits have been filed by men punished for sexual misconduct. To take one recent example, a Colgate University student was charged by an ex-girlfriend with pushing her—so hard that she fell—a year earlier. Before it even questioned the accused student, the university had already prepared a letter of interim suspension for him. He was interrogated for several hours and then told that he had been suspended; he was also offered a plane ticket home to his native Bangladesh. When the student said he wanted to stay and defend himself, security officers took him to a basement room and kept him there under guard for two days. The student was later expelled, and perhaps he did everything his ex-girlfriend alleged. But his lawsuit charges that the university simply assumed he was guilty, from the beginning, instead of taking systematic measures to determine whether he was.

Do these kinds of decisions rob the accused of their right to due process? In his recent book on sexual assault, Jon Krakauer questioned whether college disciplinary systems—even when they are arbitrary or imprecise—deprive anyone of "rights," at least in a constitutional sense; after all, he notes, university proceedings don't result in incarceration or other legal penalties. In a similar vein, a congressional lawmaker recently said that it was more important to protect students from rape than to protect students charged with it. "If there are ten people who have been accused, and under a reasonable-likelihood standard maybe one of two did it, it seems better to get rid of all ten people," declared Representative Jared Polis (D-Colorado), during a hearing on campus sexual assault. That's easy to say, of course, until you're one of the eight or nine people who are unjustly gotten rid of. But nor can schools wash their hands of the issue by turning over all sexual-assault cases to local law enforcement, as some other critics have suggested. Universities have a duty to protect their students by removing offenders from campus, and they often can't wait for the wheels of criminal justice, which simply turn too slowly. Moreover, many victims of campus sexual assault don't wish to pursue a criminal case. So while a legal investigation can and often does complement university proceedings, it can't substitute for them. At the end of the day, the university will have to police itself.[6]

So have we entered a new era of in loco parentis?

Yes and no. It's absurd to suggest—as some critics have—that the new sexual-assault policies bring us back to the era of matchbooks in the door and four legs on the floor. Those *in loco parentis* rules were designed to prevent college students—especially college women—from having sex, which was officially proscribed. That's why Vassar president Sarah Blanding announced in 1962 that if a student wished to have premarital intercourse, she should simply withdraw from college. It's impossible to imagine a university leader (outside of very religious institutions) saying any such thing today; indeed, the new sexual policing on most campuses proceeds from the assumption that students *will* have sex, not that they'll abstain. Ditto for the ever-growing list of campus rules surrounding alcohol, which has also emerged as a key focus of university attention and anxiety. Thanks to the rise in the drinking age to 21 in the 1980s, it's illegal for most undergraduates to consume alcohol. As in the case of sex, however, most universities have accepted that students will drink; instead of trying to stop it, they seek to limit its dangers. And with good reason: 40 percent of college students "binge-drink" (defined as five or more consecutive drinks for a man or four for a woman, at some point in the past two weeks), and an astonishing 2,000 students die each year from alcohol-related accidents and injuries. Heavy drinking doubles the chances of men getting into fights and also increases the risk of women experiencing sexual assault. Not surprisingly, then, "responsible drinking" has joined safe sex and affirmative consent in the pantheon of administratively promoted behaviors on American campuses.

Yet, it's also true that colleges have stepped up their overall surveillance and regulation of student life since the old *in loco parentis* regime fell away. The growing spate of regulations extend not just to sex and alcohol but also to students' speech, as we saw in Chapter 3. In part, the new rules stem from the simple wish to avoid bad press: in the era of the Internet, especially, one or two racial slurs can tar an entire institution as "unsafe" for everyone. Then there's the ever-present threat of lawsuits, and not just over sexual assault: since the 1980s, courts have increasingly allowed students and their families to sue universities for failing to protect students from any danger that the institution should have anticipated. "The fact that a college need not police the morals of its resident students . . . does not entitle it to abandon any effort to ensure their physical safety," a Massachusetts court ruled in 1983. "Parents, students, and the general community still have a reasonable expectation . . . that reasonable care will be exercised to protect resident students from foreseeable harm." Two decades later, after a student committed suicide at MIT, another state court held that her parents could sue the school for failing to take reasonable action that might have prevented her death. The parties settled out of court, but the lesson was clear: to minimize the chances of costly litigation, universities have to maximize their monitoring—and regulation—of the students in their charge.

Finally—and, to a historian, most remarkably—the increased level of oversight at our colleges also reflects the wishes of the students themselves. In most prior eras of campus unrest, students demanded less regulation and supervision from their universities; they were adults, they said, so they should be free from childlike rules and restrictions. Indeed, that's what motivated the successful campaigns against *in loco parentis* in the 1960s. But in the protests of 2015, most student demands called for more administrative action and regulation, not less. At Yale, for example, the Black Student Alliance demanded a new office to collect data about race, mandatory sensitivity trainings, and added curricular requirements. "In early every case, the students are asking to be controlled more, administered more, monitored more," wrote Mark Oppenheimer, who graduated from Yale in 1996 and returned to teach there 20 years later. "[I]t's worth asking if adding administrators and administrative requirements promotes student democracy and justice." It's also worth asking how students can grow up, if we continue to add more administrative oversight of them. We're no longer the angry biblical parent of the *in loco parentis* days, telling the kids exactly what they can and can't do. We're more like the well-meaning but overindulgent helicopter mom or dad, who keeps hovering above them instead of leaving them alone.[7]

6

HOW DID THAT MAKE
YOU FEEL?

PSYCHOLOGY AND CAMPUS POLITICS

*When did the psychology of college students become a
public issue?*

Adults have always been anxious about the well-being of
the young; in many ways, that's our job. But until the twentieth century, we worried about the rising generation's moral
and religious standing rather than its psychological health.
Founded mainly by Christian denominations, colonial-
era colleges sought to ensure that their students followed
a holy path in this world as a route to an everlasting life
thereafter. In the nineteenth century, moral character came
to replace religious piety as the central focus of concern.
Although institutions still aimed to raise good Christians,
they spoke more about instilling values of thrift, honor,
and self-discipline in young men (few women attended)
than they did about cleansing souls of sin. But the biggest
shift came in the early twentieth century, when higher education transformed from a small, confined enterprise into
a truly mass one. In the 1920s alone, student enrollment
doubled—topping 1 million for the first time—and a new
college or university opened every ten days. Roughly half
of the new students were women, and they also came from
a much wider range of religious backgrounds than before.
So did a new generation of professors, many of them

wielding Ph.D.s, who brought an increasingly scientific perspective to their research and teaching. Their watchwords were theory and evidence, not theology or morality.

So it no longer made sense for universities to promote "character," which referred to interior, subjective qualities that couldn't be measured in any kind of systematic way. Colleges instead aimed to influence student "personality," the observable and external aspect of each individual. That *could* be studied scientifically and—most of all—it could be changed, thanks to the burgeoning science of psychology. Leaving behind the ethical and religious questions that had engaged it previously, psychology reorganized as a highly quantitative, positivistic enterprise that promised to "adjust" different personalities to the changing demands of modern society. So it was tailor-made for the modern university, too. Colleges began to administer psychological tests to applicants as well as to enrolled students; they also established counseling services, to which people with "problem" personalities could be referred. Most importantly, schools developed educational programs to enhance students' psychological adjustment during their college years. Hundreds of universities established new-student orientations, where officials could "study carefully the individual problems of freshmen" and help them "meet the responsibilities and difficulties of college life," as one educator wrote. Between 50 and 60 percent of college students in the 1920s dropped out before graduating, and a third did so during their first year. With the aid of psychology, administrators hoped, they could keep these young people—and their tuition dollars—in school. As more and and more institutions entered the competition for students, there were good economic reasons to attend to their psychological health.

After World War II, meanwhile, the nation's civil rights struggle brought new attention to the psyches of a formerly neglected student population: African Americans. The Supreme Court's landmark 1954 decision in *Brown v. Board of Education* drew heavily on psychological evidence, proclaiming that the state-sponsored segregation of black schoolchildren "generates a feeling of inferiority ... that may affect their hearts and minds in a way unlikely ever to be undone." Here the Court cited the famous doll experiments by Harlem psychiatrist Kenneth B. Clark and his wife, Mamie, who found that African American children often preferred white dolls over black ones. The experiments did *not* demonstrate that this preference—which the Clarks took as a sign of low self-image—was more common in segregated schools; in fact, black kids who attended integrated schools chose white dolls more often than the African Americans at all-black institutions did.

But psychological language and argument continued to suffuse the nation's discussion of race, within both the mainstream civil rights community and more radical "Black Power" circles. Writing in 1968, Martin Luther King Jr. condemned racist school books for injuring young black psyches. "The Negro must boldly throw off the manacles of self-abnegation and say to himself and the world: 'I am somebody. I am a man with dignity and honor. I have a rich and noble history,'" King wrote. The following year, the Black Panther Party used nearly identical language in its own attack on racist textbooks. "If a man does not have knowledge of himself and his position in society and the world, then he has little chance to relate to anything else," the Panthers declared. Whatever their other differences, King and the Panthers both believed that black minds had been damaged by bigoted educational institutions. Only by reforming those institutions could African Americans restore themselves to psychological health.

Similar assumptions marked protests by black students at universities, as we saw in Chapter 3. Subjected to routine racial harassment and irrelevant coursework that ignored their historical experience, African Americans complained frequently of loneliness, alienation, and frustration. Their remedy lay in new black-oriented courses, dormitories, and centers—and also in black student activism itself, which would revive African Americans' sagging psychological strength. "[Whites] never let you forget you were black," one African American at Cal-Berkeley noted in 1967, explaining the rise of the black student union on campus, "so we decided to remember we were black." By the 1980s a flourishing field of "black psychology" had codified these experiences into a unified stage theory of African American identity, starting with self-denial and moving through rage before arriving at a healthy racial affirmation. When student protests spiked again in the late 1980s and early 1990s, especially over issues of political correctness and multiculturalism, African Africans once more invoked psychological theory and argument to demand black-oriented services and courses. This didn't represent a shift from civil rights universalism to black particularism, as many fall-from-grace histories assume. African American protesters instead demanded *both* equality across the races *and* attention to their distinct racial predicament, just as they had since the 1960s. At Stanford, for example, the president of the Black Student Union argued that the university's core reading list in Western Civilization was historically flawed, because it downplayed non-Western achievements. But it was also harmful to black students, who were injured "mentally and emotionally in ways that are not even recognized."[1]

What are microaggressions?

Indeed, many blacks observed, whites often had no idea when they were acting in a racist fashion. Writing in

1970, on the cusp of the Black Studies movement, African American psychiatrist Chester Pierce coined the term "microaggressions" to refer to subtle, unconscious insults of blacks by whites. Whereas racial slurs and other forms of direct harassment often generated the most attention and controversy, Pierce wrote, microaggressions could cause more damage in the long run. "These assaults to black dignity and hope are incessant and cumulative," Pierce warned. "In fact, the major vehicle for racism in this country is offenses done to blacks by whites in this sort of gratuitous never-ending way." If left unchallenged, seemingly minor slights could place an impossible burden on the black psyche. So schools should teach African Americans to how to identify and combat them, from the earliest possible age. "It is my fondest hope that the day is not far remote when every black child will recognize and defend promptly and adequately against every offensive microaggression," Pierce concluded.

Pierce's concept didn't get a lot of attention from academic researchers in the 1980s and 1990s. But it was revived in the early 2000s by Derald Wing Sue, a counseling psychologist who published several acclaimed books on the subject. Born in Oregon to immigrants from China, Sue was teased as a child for his ethnicity and developed a lifelong interest in questions of prejudice and discrimination. But the more he looked for overt expressions of racism, the less he could find. Modern prejudice typically took the form of oblique and indirect remarks, which led Sue back to Pierce's work on microaggression. Whereas Pierce viewed blacks as its primary victims, however, Sue saw every minority group—including his own—as a potential target. When whites asked him where he was born, Sue wrote, they sent a subtle but clear message that he was not "really" American. At least the kids on the Oregon playgrounds of his youth were open and explicit about their prejudices. But microaggression came wrapped in seemingly innocent questions and comments, which made it more insidious—and, ultimately, more destructive—than outright racism. "It is not the White supremacists, Ku Klux Klan members, or Skinheads, for example, who pose the greatest threat to people of color," Sue wrote, "but instead well-intentioned people, who are strongly motivated by egalitarian values, believe in their own morality, and experience themselves as fair-minded and decent people who would never consciously discriminate." Microaggression was the racism that knew not its name, and it was hard to get people of any race to name it.

So Sue and his collaborators proceeded to do exactly that, creating a glossary of ostensibly innocuous remarks that insulted people on the receiving end of them. Like the question about Sue's country of birth, some of the comments highlighted ethnic difference: when you ask an Asian for help with a math problem, to take another of Sue's examples, you're reinforcing the stereotype that all Asians are "good at math." Ironically, however, other microaggressions offended minorities by minimizing or ignoring their distinct heritage. "When I look at you, I don't see color" was tantamount to "denying a person of color's racial/ethnic experience," Sue wrote; likewise, "There is only one race, the human race" was "denying the individual as a racial /cultural being." By telling a minority group member that America was a "melting pot," you were implicitly instructing her to embrace "the dominant culture" instead of retaining an ethnic or racial one. If you declared that "the most qualified person should get the job," you were also announcing that "people of color are given extra unfair benefits because of their race." Finally, an employer who said, "I always treat men and women equally" was offending women by claiming to be "incapable of sexism." Depending upon who was speaking and listening, indeed, any pledge to avoid discrimination could itself represent an *act* of discrimination.[2]

How did microaggressions become a focus of campus concern?

By 2014, several universities had created websites and trainings to educate the campus community about microaggressions. Many of their theories and examples were taken directly from Derald Wing Sue, whose 2010 book was cited by University of California officials in materials prepared for a faculty leader training program to "enhance department and campus climate." Convened at nine of the ten UC campuses, the program presented Sue's complete compendium of offensive comments—including "There is only one race, the human race" and "America is a melting pot"—and explained to faculty how minority listeners might be insulted by them. At the University of Wisconsin–Stevens Point, likewise, officials reproduced a list of Sue's microaggressions—this time, drawn from a 2007 journal article—and circulated it around the school as a "discussion item" for new faculty and staff training. Wisconsin's Milwaukee campus went beyond Sue's prescriptions, widening its roster of microaggressions to include the adjective "lame" ("ridicules and ignores the lives of amputees") and the phrase "third world," which "reinforces hierarchical attitudes towards nations," according to UW–Milwaukee's Inclusive Excellence Center. The center also made national news by labeling the term "politically correct" a microaggression, on the grounds that it had "become a way to [say] that people are being too 'sensitive.'" In the age of microaggressions, it seemed, PC itself was no longer PC.

Media reports on these episodes spawned predictable cries of censorship: Since when, critics asked, did universities suppress legitimate (if controversial) political concepts like the melting pot? But nobody was banned from making microaggressive remarks, university administrators replied; their aim was not to prohibit these comments, but simply to "make people aware of how their words or actions may be interpreted when used in certain contexts," as California officials insisted. They were also responding to growing pressure from students, who were probably the main agents in transforming microaggression from an obscure academic theory into an ascending administrative concern. Whereas only 15 percent of the student demands during the November 2015 protests mentioned microaggressions by name, nearly half called for more comprehensive reporting of race-based offenses or more serious consequences for the same. And on six different campuses, students demanded that student course evaluations include items about microaggressions that had taken place in class. At Emory, for example, students asked that its end-of-semester course survey "include at least two open-ended questions" such as "Has this professor made any microaggressions towards you on account of your race, ethnicity, gender, sexual orientation, language, and/ or other identity?" and "Do you think that this professor fits into the vision of Emory University being a community of care for individuals of all racial, gender, ability and class identities?" As the students pointedly added, these questions "would help to ensure that there are repercussions or sanctions for racist actions performed by professors."

Although hard data is elusive, student charges of microaggression have surely spiked around the country over the past two years. So have accusations of "cultural appropriation," in which one group insults another by misrepresenting or caricaturing it. The issue arises most frequently in connection with Halloween costumes, which lay at the heart of the email that unleashed protests at Yale in 2015. It has also surfaced recently on Cinco de Mayo, when

Hispanic students called out people of non-Mexican descent for wearing sombreros, panchos, or fake moustaches. Others have objected to the appropriation of Mexican foods, especially the tendency for Anglos to use the shortened term "guac" for guacamole. "Guacamole is delicious. We can all agree on that," a Latina college student wrote in May 2015, on the eve of Cinco de Mayo. "But the word itself also has significance as it comes from indigenous Nahuatl language, so please make the effort to pronounce it in its entirety." Later that year, Oberlin students gained nationwide attention—and a good deal of mockery—when they complained about the inauthentic preparation of certain Asian dishes in the school cafeteria, including General Tso's chicken. "When you're cooking a country's dish for other people ... you're also representing the meaning of the dish as well as its culture," one Oberlin student told the *New York Times*. "So if people not from that heritage take food, modify it and serve it as 'authentic,' it is appropriative." Never mind that General Tso's chicken was actually developed by chefs in the United States, who tweaked an old Hunan recipe for American palates; so in this case, students were protesting the cultural appropriation of an already-appropriated dish. Nor was it clear who, exactly, was demeaned or insulted by the cuisine. As in the case of microaggressions, cultural appropriations were tabooed because they might offend certain ears, not because they necessarily did so.

And surely there were plenty of students who thought these new concerns had gone too far. Some of them were whites from conservative organizations, whose websites gleefully reprinted the more outlandish complaints about microaggressions. But other critics were members of minority groups, who felt insulted by efforts to protect them from insult. "These people do not realize that they're doing the very thing they accuse the 'victimizers' and 'oppressors' of doing—condescending to people like me," wrote a self-described Latino gay male, posting in response to a much-discussed 2015 article about micro-aggressions in the *Atlantic.* Significantly, however, he did not sign his name to his remarks. Both students and faculty members questioned microaggressions at their peril; indeed, raising doubts about the concept could constitute a microaggression in its own right, insofar as it slighted the experiences of minorities who who felt slighted. At the University of Michigan, for example, a student journalist was fired by the campus newspaper—and found his doorway pelted with eggs, hot dogs, and chewing gum—after he published a satirical column poking fun at microaggressions. Even serious-minded efforts to warn against racial microaggression could come off as racially insensitive, as Asian American students at Brandeis discovered. Seeking to raise awareness of the issue, they produced an art installation that featured examples straight out of Derald Wing Sue's playbook: Asians are good at math, I don't see race, and so on. But they were forced to remove it when other Asian students denounced the display itself as microaggressive. After that, the president of the group that had sponsored the installation circulated an email apologizing to anyone who was "triggered or hurt by the content of the microaggressions."[3]

What are trigger warnings?

Here the group's president invoked another psychological term—"trigger"—that has recently migrated into American campus politics. It refers to the painful and often unexpected reactions that a trauma victim experiences when reminded of her or his original ordeal. But whereas microaggressions had a long (albeit little-known) academic pedigree, going back nearly a half-century to the work of Chester Pierce, the trigger concept has more populist roots. Drawing on the much-discussed phenomenon of posttraumatic stress disorder among Vietnam veterans, feminist bloggers and artists in the late 1990s began to provide "trigger warnings" for any Web content that contained graphic descriptions of rape. That way, the theory went, people who had suffered sexual violence would not be forced to relive it when they encountered the topic on the Internet. Some people then started to demand or provide trigger warnings to protect victims of other types of trauma, not just sexual abuse, spawning a feisty debate in the feminist blogosphere. "Alerts have been applied to topics as diverse as sex, pregnancy, addiction, bullying, suicide, sizeism, ableism, homophobia, transphobia, slut shaming, victim-blaming, alcohol, blood, insects, small holes, and animals in wigs," one critic complained in 2014, noting that even the staid PBS hit television show "Downton Abbey" had led to requests for triggers. If all upsetting topics required a trigger, she warned, trigger warnings would lose all meaning.

Around this same time, college students also started to request trigger warnings in their classes. Here, too, demands started with a focus on sexual violence and soon encompassed a range of other subjects. At Columbia, for example, four undergraduates published an op-ed piece requesting a trigger warning for Ovid's *Metamorphoses*, a required text in the school's core curriculum, which contains a vivid description of the rape of the goddess Persephone. But that was hardly the only text in Columbia's "Great Books" roster that needed a trigger warning, as the students' op-ed also made clear. "Like so many texts in the Western cannon, [*Metamorphoses*] contains triggering and offensive material that marginalizes student identities in the classroom," the Columbia students wrote. "These texts, wrought with histories and narratives of exclusion and oppression, can be difficult to read as a survivor, a person of color, or a student from a low-income background." And since students all came from *different* backgrounds, of course, it was impossible to predict what kind of material might trigger whom. Students at Wellesley objected to a campus sculpture of a man in his underwear because it could provoke "triggering thoughts regarding sexual assault"; at Rutgers, meanwhile, one student journalist called on professors assigning F. Scott Fitzgerald's *The Great Gatsby* to include a trigger warning on the syllabus regarding "suicide, domestic abuse, and graphic violence." And at the University of California–Santa Barbara, most remarkably, student leaders passed a resolution urging the school to require trigger warnings on *all* class syllabi.

So far as we know, only one campus—the dependably left-leaning Oberlin College—instituted an official policy endorsing trigger warnings. In 2013, its website urged faculty members to "understand triggers, avoid unnecessary triggers, and provide trigger warnings." It pointedly noted that that triggers "are not only relevant to sexual misconduct, but also to anything that might cause trauma"; potential culprits included heterosexism, cissexism, and ableism as well as racism, sexism, and classism. The safest move was to purge any potentially "triggering material" from assigned readings. If a work was "too important to avoid," professors should continue to teach the text but warn students about its triggering elements beforehand. For example, the Oberlin policy cautioned, Chinua Achebe's Nobel Prize–winning *Things Fall Apart* "may trigger readers who have experienced racism, colonialism, religious persecution, violence, suicide, and more." Widely reported in the national press, many news accounts of the Oberlin policy missed the most important detail of all: that faculty objections to the policy caused Oberlin to table it before it went into effect. Most professors were actually surprised to learn about the trigger-warning initiative, which was drafted by a task force composed of one vice president, two deans, three students, two alumni, and only one faculty member (who was promoted to dean shortly after that). Like so many other recent reforms in higher education, in short, the Oberlin policy was an administrative initiative rather than a professorial one. Around the country, not surprisingly, faculty members are overwhelmingly opposed to trigger warnings. The American Association of University Professors issued a statement against trigger warnings in 2014, calling them "infantilizing and anti-intellectual." And in a 2015 survey of 800 faculty members conducted by the National Coalition Against Censorship, nearly two-thirds said trigger warnings will have a negative effect on academic freedom; almost half said they'll have a negative effect on the classroom; and only 17 percent viewed them favorably.

But over half of the surveyed faculty also said they had provided trigger warnings anyway, while nearly one-quarter said they had done so "several times" or "regularly." The reason, again, was student demand. Fifteen percent of the professors said that their students had requested trigger warnings in their courses, and half that fraction—in other words, 7.5 percent of the professors in the study—reported that students on their campus had started campaigns to require such warnings across the curriculum. Students had demanded trigger warnings about spiders, childbirth, cancer, and suicide; one appalled film professor was even asked to provide triggers before he showed bloody movie scenes in a course about horror movies! To be sure, a small fraction of professors supported trigger warnings as a way to create "a positive classroom environment" or a "safe space for dialogue," as several respondents wrote. But the vast majority were hostile to the practice, which would distort readings in the direction of the trigger itself: if you warned students about suicide in *Anna Karenina*, for example, they would inevitably focus on that subject and less on love, wealth, and the many other themes of the novel. Most of all, though, professors worried that trigger warnings—like the parietal dorm rules of old—treated adult students like children. " 'Trigger warnings' bespeak a kind of intellectual *in loco parentis* that could limit a student's opportunity for independent thinking and self-discovery," one surveyed professor complained. Indeed, another respondent observed, it allowed students to avoid any subject that they considered "uncomfortable." The world doesn't come with trigger warnings, a third professor said. Neither should college.[4]

Are today's students "coddled"?

For whatever it's worth, the president of the United States seemed to think so. Visiting an Iowa high school in 2015, Barack Obama was asked about Republican presidential candidate Ben Carson's proposal to cut off government funding from colleges exhibiting "extreme political bias." Obama replied with a ringing defense of academic freedom, calling Carson's idea "contrary to everything we believe"; indeed, Obama quipped, it was more appropriate for the former Soviet Union than for the present-day United States. But he added a warning to liberals on campus, who were guilty of their own brand of censorship. "I've heard of some college campuses where they don't want to have a guest speaker who is too conservative or they don't want to read a book if it had language that is offensive to African Americans or somehow sends a demeaning signal towards women," said Obama, a former law professor. "I've got to tell you, I don't agree with that either—that when you become students at colleges, you have to be coddled and protected from different points of view."

It's hard to know how to assess the "coddled" charge, which has wormed its way into many critiques of college students over the past several years. Students who are working part- or full-time while they go to school—and who might also be supporting children—understandably bridle at being called "coddled"; in economic terms, indeed, the current generation of college students is probably the *least* coddled cohort to ever walk onto campus. Nor is it true that all of our students—or even most of them—support trigger warnings, campaigns against microaggressions, or other efforts to shield their eyes and ears from disagreeable words or ideas. Finally, as we saw earlier, worries about psychological damage—especially to minority minds— date to the dawn of the civil rights era itself. But there's no question that today's college students are more likely to invoke the language of psychological health and illness, which has entered their political rhetoric as never before. And they're also less committed to ideals of free speech, which many students see as a potential threat to psychological health. Consider the controversy over a recent statement by faculty members on the University of Chicago's Committee on Freedom of Expression, who called for a renewed commitment to "free and open inquiry" on the nation's campuses. The statement earned accolades from civil libertarians around the country but a skeptical editorial in the *Maroon*, Chicago's student newspaper. "The report . . . implies that all speech short of unlawful harassment is acceptable, no matter how vile or cruel," the editors wrote. "While it is important for students to challenge each other's opinions, this should not come at the expense of students' mental well-being or safety."

Note the nod here not just to psychological health but to "safety," which suffuses student language on every side of the political spectrum. Students frequently complain that certain words or ideas make them feel "unsafe"; they also demand "safe spaces," where they will be protected from the same. The term originated in the 1960s and 1970s among campus feminists, who demanded woman-only (or, sometimes, feminist-only) environments where participants would be shielded from sexism and patriarchy. As in the case of trigger warnings, though, the call for safe spaces—and the indictment of unsafe ones—eventually shifted from feminists to the broader student body. It has also come to cover any number of perceived slights, which can all contribute to an "unsafe" atmosphere. At a recent Rutgers University event, for example, students smeared fake blood on themselves to protest a speech by the gay conservative blogger Milo Yiannopoulos, who blasted campuses for promoting "a culture of safe spaces and trigger warnings which seeks to insulate people from anything that might traumatize or upset them." As if to confirm his critique, protesters said Yiannopoulos should never have been invited in the first place. "[W]hat we stand for is inclusion and diversity," one student explained. "If a speaker makes someone feel unsafe or uncomfortable, then they should not come to campus."

Meanwhile, students on both sides of campus debates over Israel have decried supposed challenges to their safety. At the University of California–Santa Cruz, Jewish students charged that the Boycott, Diversity and Sanctions (BDS) campaign against Israel made them feel unsafe; in reply, a student leader in the BDS movement reported that its members—especially those of Middle Eastern descent—felt unsafe as well. And at the University of St. Thomas in Minnesota, students canceled their annual "Hump Day"—in which participants pet a camel—after critics complained that the event was cruel to animals and "insensitive" toward Middle Easterners; together, organizers said, these objections "would make for an uncomfortable and possibly unsafe environment." Gamely, some higher education leaders sought to differentiate between comfort and safety: while the university had the responsibility to keep students safe from personal attacks, Kenyon College president Sean Decatur argued, there was no equivalent duty to shield them from ideas that might make them uncomfortable. But the very need to make this distinction showed how often students were collapsing it. At Amherst, African American protesters said that campus posters calling for free speech "really affect the ability of students to be comfortable here." And at a community college in Minnesota, white students condemned a black professor for leading a class on structural racism that made *them* feel uncomfortable. "When colleges are in the business of making customers comfortable, we are all the poorer for it," one critic wrote.

She was probably right. And her choice of terms reminds us that the quest for "comfort"—like the demand for "safety"—was part of a wider consumerist revolution at our colleges, which tailor their wares to an ever-expanding clientele. Most of all, they try to construct a pleasant student experience that will retain these customers—and their tuition dollars—in a competitive marketplace. We can see that trend most strikingly in the construction of creature comforts like luxury dormitories, hot tubs, and climbing walls; at less selective institutions, especially, there's considerable evidence that student applicants choose their college based on these amenities, not on academics. And across higher education, the wish to keep customers satisfied has surely affected the way institutions try to manage the social and political environment, not just the physical one. Colleges carefully screen comedians before inviting them to campus, lest their jokes offend one constituency or another; as a journalist caustically noted, any such insult might encourage students to contemplate an "early checkout" from the "all-inclusive resort" that universities have constructed. Likewise, trigger warnings against potentially uncomfortable topics reinforce the idea that "education is a consumer experience, and that the consumers (the students) get to decide whether they like the goods on offer," as a professor told the National Coalition Against Censorship.

Other critics have blamed wider developments in American culture, especially in childrearing practices. In his best-selling 2014 critique of elite colleges, *Excellent Sheep*, former Yale professor William Deresiewicz charged that so-called helicopter parents had infantilized their children by trying to shield them from risk and danger. "Coddling and pushing, stroking and surveillance, are both forms of overprotection," he wrote. In their portrait of contemporary students, likewise, Arthur Levine and Diane Dean found them "more immature, dependent, coddled, and entitled" than students from previous eras. "This is a generation of students who have not been permitted to skin their knees," Levine and Dean wrote, borrowing another popular symbol of parental overprotection. Other observers noted rising levels of self-reported anxiety and depression among college students, which they again blamed on parents who never really let their kids become adults. If the current generation of college students is indeed "coddled," then, that's more likely the fault of the households where they grew up than the universities they attended afterwards.

Or perhaps the entire metaphor is overstated, ignoring the very real courage and commitment that our students have demonstrated. Deresiewicz and Levine and Dean both point to examples of students asking administrators if they may stage protests, which fits the "coddled" story to a T: they're so dependent on adult approval that they need permission to express disapproval. Yet most students don't wait to get clearance from college leaders before rallying against them, as we saw in November 2015; in that sense, even protests oriented toward "safe spaces" and the like reflected more risk-taking than some critics recognized. Nor have all student political activities reflected the inward, sometimes solipsistic quality of the November 2015 demonstrations. Earlier that year, for example, students at over 500 campuses organized protests urging their institutions to divest from fossil fuel companies. Harvard protesters blockaded a meeting of the board of trustees, where one undergraduate was arrested; at Yale, 19 students were. Other students demanded divestment from for-profit prison companies, earning a big win at Columbia when it became the first university to divest from such firms. At the University of Chicago, students held a sit-in to demand that the university create a medical facility for victims of gun violence in the community. And at the University of Washington, protesters demanded—and won—a raise for low-wage workers at the school. So yes, some "coddled" students demanded that the university take care of their own delicate psyches. But others were too busy fighting on behalf of others, which doesn't fit the coddled narrative at all.[5]

CONCLUSION

CAMPUS POLITICS AT THE ADMINISTRATIVE UNIVERSITY

On May 31, 1969, Wellesley College's first-ever elected class speaker delivered a short set of remarks at its 91st commencement exercises. She had been preceded at the podium by Massachusetts Senator Edward Brooke, who denounced "coercive protest" on college campuses; he also chided student demonstrators as a "curious hodge-podge" of radical elements, "irrelevant ... to the realities of American society in our time." Nonsense, the student speaker retorted. Campus protest actually contained a strong "conservative strain," which called the country back to its "old virtues"—especially, the student said, the ideal of "human liberation." By protesting America's deviations from that goal, both at home and abroad, student protesters had revived—not rejected—the nation's founding principles. And they had even set an example for the rest of the world, which was likewise struggling to implement the universal ideals at the heart of the American dream. "Every protest, every dissent ... is unabashedly an attempt to forge an identity in this particular age," she said. "It's such a great adventure. If the experiment in human living doesn't work in this country, in this age, it's not going to work anywhere."

The speaker was Hillary Diane Rodham, who would later change her name to Hillary Rodham Clinton. Her speech reminds us how much has changed—and how much has not—in campus politics over the past half-century. Like protesters today, Rodham pressed her institution to recruit and admit a more diverse array of students; her graduation speech gave a shout-out to Wellesley's new Upward Bound program, which would bring low-income high school students to campus later that summer. She also hailed several curricular changes that students had demanded and won during her college years, including a pass–fail option and a less "rigid" set of distribution requirements. Yet Rodham didn't refer directly to race or ethnicity in her speech, even in her plea to expand "the kind of people who should be coming to Wellesley." And even at an all-female college, she only mentioned women once; her other gendered references ("men with dreams," "men in the civil rights movement," "responding to men's needs") might strike many readers today as inappropriate or sexist, especially coming from a self-proclaimed feminist. At the same time, the speech also exudes a profound, almost existential optimism that feels almost as dated as its prose. Rodham didn't flinch from excoriating the "competitive corporate life" that dominated big swaths of America, "including, tragically, the universities." But she also saw college as a place where students can break out of those boundaries in their quest for a different—and better—way of being. "We are, all of us, exploring a world that none of us even understands," Rodham declared. "We're searching for more immediate, ecstatic, and penetrating modes of living."[1]

It's hard to find that spirit on college campuses today, especially in student-protest circles. Rodham's generation of students had a "love–hate relationship" with the university, as historian Robert Cohen has observed; condemning the university as a faceless and impersonal bureaucracy, they simultaneously insisted that it could also restore the lost soul of American democracy. But there's not a lot of love for

the American university among contemporary student activists; instead, there's mostly despair and disillusionment.
Unlike earlier generations of college leaders, who often
echoed Senator Brooke in denouncing student protesters,
today's university presidents embrace them. For the most
part, though, the love is unrequited. Students around the
country routinely revile university leaders as empty suits,
overly concerned with their image and out of touch with
the young people they are supposed to serve. Indeed, as
Occidental president Jonathan Veitch recently observed,
"the default mode is to be suspicious of those charged with
the responsibility of institutions." But students also expect
more of the university, even as they trust it less. On matters
of sexual assault, for example, students insist that colleges
determine the complete truth—and apply exactly the right
sanction—in matters that are often messy and ambiguous.
"It's unrealistic to think that where you have only circum-
stantial evidence, and no witnesses, that colleges are going
to be able to say with absolute clarity in every case that
they know what took place," Veitch admitted. But that's
what students expect. When they don't get it, their trust
is eroded still further; then they demand administrative
action, which inevitably falls short yet again. And so the
cycle continues.[2]

Whereas Hillary Rodham's generation typically fought
to remove administrative rules and restrictions on campus,
in short, today's students often demand more of them.
As Rodham proudly noted in her graduation speech, her
fellow students had persuaded Wellesley to reduce course
requirements and to add a pass–fail option. But contemporary protesters more often ask for increased requirements and fewer options: mandatory sensitivity trainings
for faculty, mandatory multicultural coursework for students, mandatory sexual-assault workshops at freshman
orientation, and so on. Indeed, almost every published

demand during the November 2015 protests "against" college administrations actually required *more* college administration. At Yale, where protests were triggered in part by a report that black students had been turned away from a fraternity party, students didn't organize a boycott or demonstration against the fraternity; instead, they looked to the administration to punish it. Protesters on other campuses demanded that universities hire chief diversity officers, mental health specialists, and a host of other new staffers. In the Port Huron Statement, the now-classic 1962 college protest manifesto, students resolved to "wrest control of the educational process from the administrative bureaucracy." Today they typically demand more layers of administration, which they invest with ever greater powers of bureaucratic control.[3]

That inevitably includes the regulation of speech on campus, which has become an administrative responsibility as well. And that also represents an important departure from earlier eras, when universities were called on to protect speech rather than to police it. As Senator Brooke told his audience at Wellesley, students in the late 1960s sometimes shouted down speakers or—in the most egregious cases—threatened them physically; at nearby Harvard University, for example, police had to escort Defense Secretary Robert S. McNamara from campus after protesters—screaming "murderer" and "fascist," among other epithets—surrounded his automobile. But almost nobody on campus asked universities to regulate speech; instead, they demanded that universities insure everyone's right to it. Faculty frequently took the lead in this process, drafting statements and policies to renew the university's commitment to open dialogue, discussion, and exchange. The campaign at Yale was spearheaded by historian C. Vann Woodward, who had defended communist speakers when he taught at Emory in the 1930s; moving to Scripps College during World War II, Woodward upheld the free speech rights of its German-born faculty. Then he went to Johns Hopkins, where he supported his colleague Owen Lattimore against the Red-baiting of Senator Joseph McCarthy in the 1950s. By the time Woodward got to Yale, however, the major threats to free speech came from the Left rather than from the Right. Student protesters in the early 1970s prevented General William Westmoreland from taking the podium; they also shouted down William A. Shockley, who notoriously argued that races were endowed with different levels of intelligence.

A leading scholar of American segregation and racism, Woodward was obviously appalled by Shockley's theories. But he nevertheless insisted that the university protect "freedom for the thought we hate," as per Justice Oliver Wendell Holmes's famous dictum. Like Hillary Rodham's 1969 commencement address, the 1974 Report of the Committee on Freedom of Expression at Yale—commonly known as the "Woodward Report"—has an almost antiquarian ring today, especially in its explicit elevation of free speech over every other university goal or purpose. The report acknowledged the "shock, hurt, and anger" that can result from hateful speech, including "slurs and epithets intended to discredit another's race, ethnic group, religion, or sex." But the university was a "place for knowledge," which required a full and free exchange of ideas in order to thrive and grow. And that value took precedence over every other one, including the cultivation of interracial tolerance and harmony. "It may sometimes be necessary in a university for civility and mutual respect to be superseded by the need to guarantee free expression," the Woodward Report concluded. The contest between free speech and civility was no contest at all; at a university, free speech should win out every time.[4]

Today, by contrast, civility takes first place. The shift began with the promulgation of campus speech codes in the late 1980s, following a series of highly publicized racial incidents. Since then, as we saw in Chapter 3, universities have developed an elaborate set of checks and controls on expression that might insult, threaten, or offend minority groups. The most obvious reason was the steady increase in enrollment of minorities themselves, in response to demands like the one Hillary Rodham issued in her graduation speech. Whereas Rodham and her generation imagined that greater racial diversity would lead to a corresponding increase in interracial tolerance and understanding, however, campus experience told a different story. Among white students, appreciation of diversity was often—to use a very loaded metaphor—skin deep: students routinely gave rhetorical assent to the concept but rarely engaged seriously or deeply with classmates of other backgrounds. And as the November 2015 protests confirmed, over and over again, many minority students came to see the entire diversity project as something of a sham: designed primarily to burnish institutions' image, it didn't serve or accommodate students of color in a meaningful or substantial way. On most campuses, then, students of different races were more likely to talk past each other than with each other. As early as 1990, a major study of diversity at the proudly multiethnic University of California at Berkeley found that minority students felt "ignored or excluded" while whites "felt like they were walking on eggshells, always afraid of being called 'racist.'" Into the present, students maintain a "sanitized and superficial tolerance" across their differences, as sociologist Mary Grigsby has observed. More than anything else, they seek to avoid "open conflicts about serious matters of difference in public spaces."[5]

That's the only way to understand the continued growth and apparent popularity of speech codes, which help our students navigate the dangerous shoals of American diversity. Most students seem to approve of these regulations or at least to acquiesce in them; indeed, it's hard to imagine how universities could have retained or expanded speech codes—even in the face of court decisions ruling them unconstitutional—without a healthy dose of student support. As several recent surveys confirm, young Americans are now more likely to advocate curbs on free speech than older Americans are. Whereas 34 percent of Americans say the First Amendment "goes too far" in protecting individual rights, 47 percent of people aged 18–32 hold that that view. And 60 percent of Americans in their 20s say that Muslim clergymen "who preach hatred against the United States" should not be allowed to do so publicly in their community, as compared to 53 percent of Americans in their 30s and 43 percent in their 40s.

Most alarmingly, to advocates of free speech on campus, college students might be even less tolerant than other members of their age cohort. A nationwide survey of freshmen in 2015–2016 found that 71 percent agreed that "colleges should prohibit racist/sexist speech on campus," up from 59 percent in 1992. And 43 percent of respondents said that colleges should have the right to ban "extreme speakers" from campus, compared to just 25 percent in 1971. There's also some evidence that young people today are less adept than earlier generations at face-to-face communication, which might also help explain their support for the regulation of it. Over half of community college students and a third of four-year students agree with the statement that "I pretty much keep to myself socially"; across our campuses, increasingly, students prefer the anonymity of the Internet to the messy, unpredictable labor of in-person interaction. Even phone calls are avoided in favor of texting, which makes students feel more control over the exchange—and less anxiety about its outcome.[6]

These new technologies also make it easier to "flame" at others—that is, to send inappropriate and injudicious messages that you'd probably never deliver in person. And that brings us to a troubling paradox at the heart of campus politics: despite its ostensible emphasis on "civility," it has also generated profoundly uncivil behavior. Most of that takes place in the netherworld of social media, out of the purview of the people who run the institutions. But it has also influenced in-person interactions, where the university's overriding emphasis on preventing slights has (again, paradoxically) given people license to flame when they feel slighted. Witness the bitter confrontation at Yale, where an African American student was caught on camera shrieking at a house master, "You should not sleep at night! You are disgusting!" Or consider the fact that universities have seen more than 240 campaigns to block visiting speakers from campus since 2000, many of them targeted at people considered insensitive toward minorities. Meanwhile, over the same time period, student media have reported over 250 incidents of newspaper theft. Some of the papers were stolen because students found their reporting racially offensive; in other cases, one group of students simply wanted to avoid being criticized by another. In Texas, a football coach actually praised his team for stealing the entire press run of a student paper that reported on the arrest of one of his players. "I'm proud of my players for doing that," the coach said. "This was the best team building exercise we have ever done."[7]

That speaks volumes about the challenges to free speech on campus. The coach wasn't wrong about the ways that censoring others can bind a group together; as Justice Holmes wrote, in a passage that C. Vann Woodward also quoted, it was "perfectly logical" to "sweep away all opposition" in the quest for moral victory. But it was also destructive, because it prevented the intellectual back-and-forth that would yield—in the end—a higher truth than your own team's. What our campuses need now is a revival of Woodward's ideal, to remind all of us about why it matters. As we saw in Chapter 4, professors have done an admirable job protecting their own free speech rights from different challenges in the post-9/11 era. But we've been less vigilant about demanding the same rights for our students, no matter what they are saying or who might be listening. One admirable exception was the 2015 report issued by the University of Chicago's Committee on Freedom of Expression, which echoed the Woodward Report in its explicit prizing of free exchange over every other principle. "Although the University greatly values civility," the report declared, "concerns about civility and mutual respect can never be used as a justification for closing off discussion of ideas, however offensive or disagreeable those ideas may be to some members of our community." The goal of civility has created an often uncivil environment, where people either censor their own opinions—for fear of causing offense—or muzzle others. The best route to real civility turns out to be free speech, which teaches us how to disagree across our differences instead of keeping silent about them.[8]

And we have plenty of examples from recent campus politics, where students have engaged in rich debates about extremely difficult topics. Free speech *is* under fire at our universities, but it's hardly snuffed out. Consider recent battles over Boycott, Diversity and Sanctions (BDS) resolutions against Israel, which have sparked accusations of hate speech on every side: Jewish groups decry expressions of anti-Semitism by BDS supporters, who charge that they have been maligned because of their Islamic or Middle Eastern background. The exchange has been loud, impassioned, and, yes, sometimes hateful: on one California campus, for example, BDS advocates displayed posters equating Zionism with Nazism and an Israeli flag dripping with blood. Jewish students eventually complained to the Department of Education's Office of Civil Rights (OCR), claiming their institutions hadn't done enough to protect them from a "hostile environment" on campus. But the OCR issued a welcome rebuff to the students' plea, noting that "exposure to such robust and discordant expressions, even when personally offensive and hurtful, is a circumstance that a reasonable student in higher education may experience." That's not to minimize or deny the very real presence of anti-Semitism at our universities: in a recent survey of 1,000 Jewish students on 55 campuses, for example, over half reported experiencing or witnessing an anti-Semitic act or comment in the previous six months. Why should racist or sexist comments draw penalties from universities, some Jewish students asked, while anti-Semitic ones don't? It's a good question, but the answer isn't to replace one error with another. Our courts have ruled that all kinds of hate speech are protected, no matter whom they target. It's time for our universities to follow suit.[9]

And it's time for our students to step up, too, and start leveraging their own power instead of investing yet more of it in university administrations. If a fraternity holds a racist party, don't look to the college president to shut it down; boycott every event at fraternity, and urge your friends to do the same. If students aren't learning enough about diversity, don't demand yet another course requirement (at yet more cost to you, the tuition-payer); hold a teach-in yourselves, bringing in the texts and themes that the official curriculum is neglecting. If there's a spike in sexual assault on campus, don't rely on university officials to eliminate it; protest instead outside of the dorms, reminding everyone about what goes on inside of them. If you dislike something published in the campus newspaper, don't ask the university to cut its funding (and please, don't steal the paper!); produce your own online journals and blogs, and circulate them far and wide. And if you want gender-neutral bathrooms, to better accommodate transgender students, don't wait for some administrator to create them; just walk around campus and post all-gender signs on bathroom doors, as protesters have been doing at several universities in recent years.

It's also worth remembering how apolitical most of our colleges remain, despite the recent burst of protest at a small subset of mostly selective ones. Even at institutions that have witnessed demonstrations, we tend to exaggerate students' overall level of political engagement and to assume—against all evidence—that they all lean to the hard left. But going back to 1990, at the start of the panic over political correctness, two-thirds of Harvard students supported America's invasion of Iraq in the first Gulf War; that was actually a greater fraction than the proportion of the overall citizenry who backed the war. Fully half of recent graduates from Harvard and the University of Pennsylvania have entered consulting or finance, hardly known as hotbeds of radical sentiment. But students at elite schools *are* more liberal than the average undergraduate, which helps explain why protests have have been rare at community colleges and other nonselective public institutions. So does that fact that students at these schools tend to be older and often work part-time or even full-time, which obviously cuts down on the energy and attention they can devote to student politics. No matter where they study, finally, economic insecurity seems to have made students less concerned about the common-weal and more worried about themselves. Eighty-two percent of college freshmen say that "becoming very well-off financially" is an important goal to them, up from 42 percent in 1966. Students go to college to get ahead, which usually means leaving politics behind.[10]

But that might be changing, too, precisely because America's growing student body feels so economically squeezed. Community colleges and nonselective regional institutions dominated the list of 150 schools that witnessed student walkouts during the 2011 "Occupy Colleges" protests, which were focused mainly on student tuition and debt; indeed, as Arthur Levine and Diane Dean recently observed, the Occupy walkouts "may have been historically unique for being populated by students in the mass rather than elite sector of higher education." Students at nonselective colleges have also led the battle against their schools' agreements with credit credit card companies, which allegedly enrich the colleges even as they fleece individual borrowers. Other students at America's sprawling universities—which University of California president Clark Kerr famously said were "held together by a common grievance over parking"—have found themselves called before speech tribunals for using intemperate or offensive language in complaints about parking spaces and tickets. And they're fighting back, too, questioning the right of a public college to restrict criticism of itself. That hardly signals a revolution, of course, but it's a start. As Hillary Rodham told her own graduating class, nearly a half-century ago, campus politics is a great adventure. And we are, all of us, exploring a world that none of us really understands.[11]

NOTES

Introduction

1. Emma Pierson and Leah Pierson, "What Do Campus Protesters Really Want?," *New York Times*, December 9, 2015, at http://kristof.blogs.nytimes.com/2015/12/09/what-do-campus-protesters-really-want/, accessed January 24, 2016; "Amherst Uprising: What We Stand For," November 13, 2015, at http://www.amherstsoul.com/post/133122838315/amherst-uprising-what-we-stand-for, accessed January 25, 2016; "Demands of Black Voices: Presented at 'Duke Tomorrow' on November 20th, 2015," at http://static1.squarespace.com/static/541e2ec8e4b042b085c464d9/t/56515dfae4b033f56d2481bc/1448173050985/dukedemands.pdf, accessed January 25, 2016.

2. Jailyn Gladney, "Boston University Is Proof That University Campuses Are Anything but 'Post-Racial,'" *StudentNation*, July 14, 2015, at http://www.thenation.com/article/boston-university-is-proof-that-university-campuses-are-anything-but-post-racial/, accessed January 25, 2016.

3. Randall Kennedy, "Black Tape at Harvard Law," *New York Times*, November 27, 2015, p. A31.

4. "Students Rally with List of Demands for Purdue," *Purdue Exponent*, November 14, 2015, at http://www.purdueexponent.org/campus/article_9a40a5c2-8b40-11e5-9437-53fbc13874e0.html, accessed January 24, 2016.

5. Robert Cohen, "The New Left's Love-Hate Relationship with the University," in *The Port Huron Statement: Sources and Legacies of the New Left's Founding Manifesto*, ed. Richard Flacks and Nelson Lichtenstein (Philadelphia: University of Pennsylvania Press, 2015), 118–119; "Yale President Tells Minority Students: 'We Failed You,'" *Washington Post*, November 6, 2015, at https://www.washingtonpost.com/news/grade-point/wp/2015/11/06/yales-president-tells-black-students-we-failed-you/, accessed January 26, 2016.

Chapter 1

1. Neil Gross, "The Social and Political Views of American College and University Professors," in *Professors and their Politics*, ed. Neil Gross and Solon Simmons (Baltimore: Johns Hopkins University Press, 2015), 36–38, 31, 24–25; Neil Gross, *Why Are Professors Liberal and Why Do Conservatives Care?* (Cambridge, MA: Harvard University Press, 2013), 27–28, 9, 46, 183–184; Sam Abrams, "Professors Moved Left Since 1990s, Rest of Country Did Not," *Heterodox Academy*, January 9, 2016, at http://heterodoxacademy.org/2016/01/09/professors-moved-left-but-country-did-not/, accessed January 18, 2016.

2. Gross, *Why Are Professors Liberal*, 122, 91–92, 223, 230, 232, 236; Jon A. Shields and Joshua M. Dunn, *Passing on the Right: Conservative Professors in the Progressive Academy* (New York: Oxford University Press, 2016), 69, 84, 100–101, 83, 92, 109, 125; "Punch Lines Versus Polish on Iowa Trail," *New York Times*, January 1, 2016, p. A1; Conor Friedersdorf, "Ben Carson Calls for Right-Wing Fairness Doctrine on College Campuses," *Atlantic*, October 22, 2015, at http://www.theatlantic.com/politics/archive/2015/10/ben-carson-calls-for-a-right-wing-fairness-doctrine-on-college-campuses/411865/, accessed January 8, 2016.

3. Helen Horowitz, *Campus Life: Undergraduate Cultures from the End of the Eighteenth Century to the Present* (Chicago: University of Chicago Press, 1988), 223; Amy J. Binder and Kate Wood, *Becoming Right: How Campuses Shape Young Conservatives* (Princeton, NJ: Princeton University Press, 2013), 33–35; Arthur Levine and Diane R. Dean, *Generation on a Tightrope: A Portrait of Today's*

College Student, 3rd ed. (San Francisco: Jossey-Bass, 2012), 130, 136–137; Richard Arum and Josipa Roksa, *Aspiring Adults Adrift: Tentative Transitions of College Graduates* (Chicago: University of Chicago Press, 2014), 103, 99; David T. Z. Mindich, "A Wired Nation Turns Out the News," in *The State of the American Mind*, ed. Mark Bauerlein and Adam Bellow (Conshohocken, PA: Templeton Press, 2015), 99; American Council of Trustees and Alumni, "Survey Reveals Pervasive Political Pressure in the Classroom," *FrontPageMag.com*, December 9, 2004, at http://archive.frontpagemag.com/readArticle.aspx?ARTID=10267, accessed January 9, 2016; Kyle Dodson, "The Effect of College on Social and Political Attitudes and Civic Participation," in *Professors and their Politics*, ed. Gross and Simmons, 149, 156; Richard Arum and Josipa Roksa, *Academically Adrift: Limited Learning on College Campuses* (Chicago: University of Chicago Press, 2011), 8, 3.

4. Horowitz, *Campus Life*, 221; Christopher J. Broadhurst, "Campus Activists in the 21st Century: A Historical Framing," in *"Radical Academia"? Understanding the Climates for Campus Activists*, ed. Christopher J. Broadhurst and Georgianna L. Martin (San Francisco: Jossey-Bass, 2014), 10; Robert A. Rhoads, *Freedom's Web: Student Activism in an Age of Cultural Diversity* (Baltimore: Johns Hopkins University Press, 1998), 39; Levine and Dean, *Generation on a Tightrope*, 126, 54, 121; Angus Johnston, "Student Protests, Then and Now," *Chronicle of Higher Education* 62 (December 18, 2015): 13; George Yancey, "Disrespect, Intimidation, and Prejudice at the University of Colorado," *Patheos*, December 21, 2014, at http://www.patheos.com/blogs/blackwhiteandgray/2014/12/disrespect-intimidation-and-prejudice-at-the-university-of-colorado/, accessed January 6, 2016; Binder and Wood, *Becoming Right*, 3, 156.

Chapter 2

1. Geoffrey Hughes, *Political Correctness: A History of Semantics and Culture* (Malden, MA: Blackwell, 2010), 62–64, 24; Ruth Perry, "A Short History of the Term *Politically Correct*," in *Beyond PC: Toward a Politics of Understanding*, ed. Patricia Aufderheide (St. Paul, MN: Graywolf, 1992), 71–72, 75.

2. Lawrence W. Levine, *The Unpredictable Past: Explorations in American Cultural History* (New York: Oxford University Press, 1993), 7–8; Andrew Hartman, *A War for the Soul of America: A History of the Culture Wars* (Chicago: University of Chicago Press, 2015), 223–224; Allan Bloom, *The Closing of the American Mind* (New York: Simon & Schuster, 1987), 320, 337; Ellen Schrecker, *The Lost Soul of Higher Education: Corporatization, the Assault on Academic Freedom, and the End of the American University* (New York: New Press, 2010), 89–90.

3. Hartman, *War for the Soul of America*, 227–230, 243; "Thought Police," *Newsweek*, December 24, 1990, pp. 48–55; Michael Berube, "Public Image Limited: Political Correctness and the Media's Big Lie," in *Debating P.C.: The Controversy over Political Correctness on College Campuses*, ed. Paul Berman (New York: Delta, 1995), 135; Dinesh D'Souza, *Illiberal Education: The Politics of Race and Sex on Campus* (New York: Free Press, 1991), 239; George Bush, "Remarks at the University of Michigan Commencement Ceremony in Ann Arbor," May 4, 1991, at http://www.presidency.ucsb.edu/ws/?pid=19546, accessed January 20, 2016. John K. Wilson reported 29 uses of the acronym "PC" in the 1990 *Newsweek* article, but my own count was 27. *The Myth of Political Correctness: The Conservative Attack on Higher Education* (Durham, NC: Duke University Press, 1995), 13–14.

4. Jonathan Zimmerman, "Foreword," in *Political Correctness and Higher Education: British and American Perspectives*, ed. John Lea (New York: Routledge, 2009), vii; Schrecker, *Lost Soul of Higher Education*, 101–104; Barbara Ehrenreich, "The Challenge for the Left," in Berman, ed., *Debating P.C.*, 335; Robert Hughes, *The Culture of Complaint* (New York: Oxford University Press), 18–19; Jonathan Zimmerman, "Republican Hopefuls Playing Politics with Science," *San Francisco Chronicle*, August 31, 2011, at http://www.sfgate.com/opinion/openforum/article/Republican-hopefuls-playing-politics-with-science-2333168.php, accessed January 10, 2016; Barbara Epstein, "Political Correctness and Identity Politics," in Aufderheide, ed., *Beyond P.C.*, 153–154, 149; Russell Jacoby, *Dogmatic*

Wisdom (New York: Doubleday, 1994), 49, 82; Richard J. Ellis, *The Dark Side of the Left: Illiberal Egalitarianism in America* (Lawrence: University Press of Kansas, 1998), 221–222.

5. Jacoby, *Dogmatic Wisdom*, 6–8; Richard A. Settersten Jr., "The New Landscape of Adulthood: Implications for Broad-Access Higher Education," in *Remaking College: The Changing Ecology of Higher Education*, ed. Michael W. Kirst and Mitchell L. Stevens (Stanford, CA: Stanford University Press, 2015), 124; Regina Deil-Amen, "The 'Traditional' College Student: A Smaller and Smaller Minority and Its Implications for Diversity and Access Institutions," in Kirst and Stevens, eds., *Remaking College*, 147; Hartman, *War for the Soul of America*, 288–289; Greg Lukianoff, "How Colleges Create 'Expectation Confirmation,'" in *The State of the American Mind*, ed. Mark Bauerlein and Adam Bellow (Conshohocken, PA: Templeton Press, 2015), 210; Lukianoff, *Unlearning Liberty: Campus Censorship and the End of American Debate* (New York: Encounter, 2014 [2012]), 56.

Chapter 3

1. Goldie Blumenstyk, *American Higher Education in Crisis?* (New York: Oxford University Press, 2015), 13–15, 27–35; Richard D. Kahlenberg, *Achieving Better Diversity: Reforming Affirmative Action in Higher Education* (New York: The Century Foundation, 2015), 15; "Affirmative Action Ban at UC, 15 Years Later," *San Jose Mercury News*, June 24, 2013, at http://www.mercurynews.com/ci_23516740/affirmative-action-ban-at-uc-15-years-later, accessed January 7, 2016; National Center for Education Statistics, "Fast Facts," at http://nces.ed.gov/fastfacts/display.asp?id=61, accessed January 18, 2016; Conor Friedersdorf, "Does Affirmative Action Create Mismatches Between Students and Universities?," *Atlantic*, December 15, 2015, at http://www.theatlantic.com/politics/archive/2015/12/the-needlessly-polarized-mismatch-theory-debate/420321/, accessed February 20, 2016; Julia Lurie, "Just How Few Professors of Color Are at America's Top Colleges?," *Mother Jones*, November 23, 2015, at http://www.motherjones.com/politics/

2015/11/university-faculty-diversity-race-gender-charts, accessed January 4, 2016; Mary Ann Mason, "The Pyramid Problem," *Chronicle of Higher Education*, March 9, 2011, at http://chronicle.com/article/The-Pyramid-Problem/126614/, accessed December 30, 2015; Walter M. Kimbrough, "Black College Students Demanding More Black Professors Don't Realize 'They Are Demanding the Impossible,'" *Atlanta Journal-Constitution*, December 21, 2015, at http://getschooled.blog.myajc.com/2015/12/21/black-college-students-demanding-more-black-professors-dont-realize-they-are-demanding-the-impossible/, accessed January 3, 2016.

2. Lisa M. Stulberg and Anthony S. Chen, "A Long View on 'Diversity': A Century of American College Admissions Debates," in *Diversity in American Higher Education: Toward a More Comprehensive Approach*, ed. Lisa M. Stulberg and Sharon L. Weinberg (New York: Routledge, 2011), 54, 59; Christopher P. Loss, *Between Citizens and the State: The Politics of American Higher Education in the Twentieth Century* (Princeton, NJ: Princeton University Press, 2011), 176–177, 192, 195; Ellen Schrecker, *The Lost Soul of Higher Education: Corporatization, the Assault on Academic Freedom, and the End of the American University* (New York: New Press, 2010), 78, 80; Julie A. Reuben, "Merit, Mission, and Minority Students: The History of the Debate over Special Admissions Programs," in *A Faithful Mirror: Reflections on the College Board and Education in America*, ed. Michael Johanek (New York: College Board, 2001), 216–218; Martha Biondi, *The Black Revolution on Campus* (Berkeley: University of California Press, 2012), 4, 18–22; Fabio Rojas, "Activism and the Academy: Lessons from the Rise of Ethnic Studies," in *Professors and Their Politics*, ed. Neil Gross and Solon Simmons (Baltimore: Johns Hopkins University Press, 2014), 248.

3. *Regents of the University of California v. Bakke*, 438 U.S. 265 (1978); Reuben, "Merit, Mission, and Minority Students, " 231; Jonathan Zimmerman, "What Happened to Freedom of Speech?," *Inside Higher Ed*, April 13, 2015, at https://www.insidehighered.com/views/2015/04/13/essay-criticizes-colleges-expelling-students-racist-comments, accessed December 22, 2015; Timothy C. Shiell, *Campus Hate Speech on Trial*, 2nd ed. (Lawrence: University Press

of Kansas, 2009), 17–21, 47; Donald Alexander Downs, *Restoring Free Speech and Liberty on Campus* (Cambridge, UK: Cambridge University Press, 2005), 52; Schrecker, *Lost Soul of Higher Education*, 111; Greg Lukianoff, *Unlearning Liberty: Campus Censorship and the End of American Debate* (New York: Encounter, 2014 [2012]), 41, 48–50; Jonathan Zimmerman, "Expulsion for Language, Not for Sexual Assault?," *New York Daily News*, March 11, 2015, at http://www.nydailynews.com/opinion/jonathan-zimmerman-ou-dangerous-double-standard-article-1.2145773, accessed December 20, 2016.

4. Debbie Bazarsky and Ronni Sanlo, "LGBT Students, Faculty, and Staff: Past, Present, and Future Directions," in Stulberg and Weinberg, eds., *Diversity in American Higher Education*, 131–132; Anthony Lising Antonio and Chris Gonzalez Clarke, "The Official Organization of Diversity in American Higher Education," ibid., 88; Schrecker, *Lost Soul of Higher Education*, 178; Andrew Kelly, "The Real Winners in Campus Protests? College Administrators," *Forbes*, November 24, 2015, at http://www.forbes.com/sites/akelly/2015/11/24/the-real-winners-in-campus-protests-college-ad-ministrators/#1c27be54c2e4, accessed December 24, 2015; Conor Friedersdorf, "Brown University's $100 Million Inclusivity Plan," *Atlantic*, November 24, 2015, at http://www.theatlantic.com/politics/archive/2015/11/brown-universitys-100-million-plan-to-be-more-inclusive/416886/, accessed January 3, 2016; Loss, *Between Citizens and the State*, 229–231; Beth McMurtrie, "One Campus Approaches Diversity Training with 'Hard Data and Careful Thought,'" *Chronicle of Higher Education*, November 20, 2015, at http://chronicle.com/article/One-Campus-Approaches/234281, accessed December 28, 2016; Steve Kolowich, "Diversity Training in Demand: Does It Work?," *Chronicle of Higher Education* 62 (November 20, 2015): A6; Elisabeth Lasch-Quinn, *Race Experts: How Racial Etiquette, Sensitivity Training, and New Age Therapy Hijacked the Civil Rights Revolution* (New York: Norton, 2001), 163; Leah Libresco, "Here Are the Demands from Students Protesting Racism at 51 Colleges," *fivethirtyeight.com*, December 3, 2015, at http://fivethirtyeight.com/features/here-are-

the-demands-from-students-protesting-racism-at-51-colleges/, accessed January 24, 2016; Emma Pierson and Leah Pierson, "What Do Campus Protesters Really Want?," *New York Times,* December 9, 2015, at http://kristof.blogs.nytimes.com/2015/12/09/what-do-campus-protesters-really-want/, accessed January 24, 2016; Benjamin Ginsberg, *The Fall of the Faculty: The Rise of the All-Administrative University and Why It Matters* (New York: Oxford University Press, 2011), 111–115.

5. Arthur Levine and Diane R. Dean, *Generation on a Tightrope: A Portrait of Today's College Student,* 3rd ed. (San Francisco: Jossey-Bass, 2012), 99–102, 107; Sarah Brown, "Diversity Courses Are in High Demand: Can They Make a Difference?," *Chronicle of Higher Education* 62 (January 7, 2016): 15; Jim Sidanius, Shana Levin, Colette Van Laar, and David O. Sears, *The Diversity Challenge: Social Identity and Intergroup Relations on the College Campus* (New York: Russell Sage, 2008), 322–323; Kolowich, "Diversity Training in Demand"; Scott Jaschik, "What the Protests Mean," *Inside Higher Ed,* November 16, 2015, at https://www.insidehighered.com/news/2015/11/16/experts-consider-what-protests-over-racial-tensions-mean, accessed January 24, 2016; Jaschik, "Escalating Demands," *Inside Higher Ed,* December 3, 2015, at https://www.insidehighered.com/news/2015/12/03/student-protest-lists-demands-get-longer-and-more-detailed, accessed January 24, 2106; Mitchell L. Stevens, *Creating a Class: College Admissions and the Education of an Elite* (Cambridge, MA: Harvard University Press, 2009), 176–177.

Chapter 4

1. "Florida professor who cast doubt on mass shootings is fired," *New York Times,* January 6, 2016, p. A15; Scott Jaschik, "University Moves to Fire Sandy Hook Denier," *Inside Higher Ed,* December 17, 2015, at https://www.insidehighered.com/news/2015/12/17/florida-atlantic-moves-fire-sandy-hook-denier, accessed December 29, 2015; American Association of University Professors, "1915 Declaration of Principles on Academic Freedom and Academic Tenure," at http://www.aaup.org/NR/

rdonlyres/A6520A9D-0A9A-47B3-B550-C006B5B224E7/0/
1915Declaration.pdf, accessed January 20, 2016.

2. Ellen Schrecker, *The Lost Soul of Higher Education: Corporatization, the Assault on Academic Freedom, and the End of the American University* (New York: New Press, 2010), 44–46, 37, 25; Louis Menand, *The Marketplace of Ideas: Reform and Resistance in the American University* (New York: Norton, 2010), 130; Philippa Strum, "Why Academic Freedom? The Theoretical and Constitutional Context," in *Academic Freedom after September 11*, ed. Beshara Doumani (New York: Zone, 2006), 145–149; Neil Gross, *Why Are Professors Liberal and Why Do Conservatives Care?* (Cambridge, MA: Harvard University Press, 2013), 25.

3. Beshara Doumani, "Between Coercion and Privatization: Academic Freedom in the Twenty-First Century," in Doumani, ed., *Academic Freedom After September 11*, 11; Marjorie Heins, *Priests of Our Democracy: The Supreme Court, Academic Freedom, and the Anti-Communist Purge* (New York: New York University, 2013), 256–260; Joel Beinin, "The New McCarthyism: Policing Thought About the Middle East," in Doumani, ed., *Academic Freedom After September 11*, 244–245, 253–254; David K. Shipler, *Rights at Risk: The Limits of Liberty in Modern America* (New York: Knopf, 2012), 293–295.

4. Schrecker, *Lost Soul of Higher Education*, 125–142; Adam Chandler, "A Six-Figure Settlement on Campus Free Speech," *Atlantic*, November 12, 2015, at http://www.theatlantic.com/national/archive/2015/11/a-six-figure-settlement-on-campus-free-speech/415680/, accessed January 21, 2016; Tammi Rossman-Benjamin, "Interrogating the Academic Boycotters of Israel on American Campuses," in *The Case Against Academic Boycotts*, ed. Cary Nelson and Gabriel Noah Brahm (Chicago: Modern Language Association Members for Scholars' Rights, 2015), 218–220; Elizabeth Redden, "Middle East Conflict, U.S. Campuses," *Inside Higher Ed*, June 17, 2014, at https://www.insidehighered.com/news/2014/06/17/pro-palestinian-student-activism-heats-causing-campus-tensions, accessed January 21, 2016; Elizabeth Redden, "Big Night for Boycott Movement," *Inside Higher Ed*,

November 23, 2015, at https://www.insidehighered.com/news/ 2015/11/23/anthropologists-overwhelmingly-vote-boycott-israeli-universities, accessed January 21, 2016; "AAUP Statement on Academic Boycotts," May 10, 2013, at http://www.aaup.org/ news/aaup-statement-academic-boycotts, accessed January 21, 2016.

5. William F. Buckley Jr. and L. Brent Bozell, *McCarthy and His Enemies: The Record and Its Meaning* (New York: Regnery, 1954), 132; Cary Nelson, "The Fragility of Academic Freedom," in Nelson and Brahm, eds., *The Case Against Academic Boycotts,* 66; "AAUP's Letter to FAU's President Saunders," April 16, 2013, at http:// www.aaup.org/news/aaups-letter-faus-president-saunders, accessed January 6, 2016; Conor Friedersdorf, "How Sexual-Harassment Policies Are Diminishing Academic Freedom," *Atlantic,* October 20, 2015, at http://www.theatlantic.com/politics/archive/ 2015/10/sexual-harassment-academic-freedom/411427/, accessed January 22, 2016; Geoffrey Stone and Will Creely, "Restoring Free Speech on Campus," *Washington Post,* September 25, 2015, at https:// www.washingtonpost.com/opinions/restoring-free-speech-on-campus/2015/09/25/65d58666-6243-11e5-8e9e-dce8a2a2a679_story. html, accessed January 22, 2016; Sara Lipka, "An Arc of Outrage," *Chronicle of Higher Education* 61 (April 13, 2015): 26; Benjamin Ginsberg, *The Fall of the Faculty: The Rise of the All-Administrative University and Why It Matters* (New York: Oxford University Press, 2011), 160; Schrecker, *Lost Soul of Higher Education,* 213–215; Edward Schlosser, "I'm a Liberal Professor, and My Liberal Students Terrify Me," *Vox,* June 3, 2015, at http://www.vox.com/2015/6/3/8706323/ college-professor-afraid, accessed January 22, 2016.

Chapter 5

1. Christopher P. Loss, *Between Citizens and the State: The Politics of American Higher Education in the Twentieth Century* (Princeton, NJ: Princeton University Press, 2011), 36–37; Beth Bailey, "Sexual Revolution(s)," in *The Sixties: From Memory to History,* ed. David Farber (Chapel Hill: University of North Carolina Press, 1994), 241; Jonathan Zimmerman, "Sex Drive Blurs Line

Surrounding Assault," *USA Today,* November 24, 2013, at http://
www.usatoday.com/story/opinion/2013/11/24/sex-rape-uconn-
assault-college-campus-column/3693219/, accessed January 9,
2016; Eleanore Rowland Wembridge, "Petting and the Campus,"
Survey 54 (July 1, 1925): 393.

2. Bailey, "Sexual Revolution(s)," 250–252; B. Richardson and
   J. Shields, "The Real Campus Assault Problem—and How to Fix
   It," *Commentary,* October 1, 2015, at https://www.commentary-
   magazine.com/articles/real-campus-sexual-assault-problem-fix/,
   accessed January 9, 2016; Loss, *Between Citizens and the State,* 36–37,
   209–210.

3. "She Can Play That Game, Too," *New York Times,* July 14, 2013, p. ST1;
   Elizabeth A. Armstrong and Laura T. Hamilton, *Paying for the
   Party: How College Maintains Inequality* (Cambridge, MA: Harvard
   University Press, 2013), 86; Arthur Levine and Diane R. Dean,
   Generation on a Tightrope: A Portrait of Today's College Student, 3rd
   ed. (San Francisco: Jossey-Bass, 2012), 64–67; Daniel Reimold, *Sex
   and the University: Celebrity, Controversy, and A Student Journalism
   Revolution* (New Brunswick, NJ: Rutgers University Press, 2010),
   11–12, 19–22, 4, 124, 130; Amy J. Binder and Kate Wood, *Becoming
   Right: How Campuses Shape Young Conservatives* (Princeton,
   NJ: Princeton University Press, 2013), 285–286.

4. Zimmerman, "Sex Drive Blurs Line Surrounding Assault"; John
   J. Sloan III and Bonnie S. Fisher, *The Dark Side of the Ivory Tower:
   Campus Crime as a Social Problem* (Cambridge, UK: Cambridge
   University Press, 2011), 87–94; Donald Alexander Downs, *Restoring
   Free Speech and Liberty on Campus* (Cambridge, UK: Cambridge
   University Press, 2005), 86–88, 97; Jonathan Zimmerman,
   "Duke Lacrosse Players Not Exactly Role Models," *Philadelphia
   Inquirer,* June 20, 2007, at http://articles.philly.com/2007-06-20/
   news/25233708_1_lacrosse-players-strip-club-michael-b-nifong,
   accessed January 9, 2016; Jon Krakauer, *Missoula: Rape and the
   Justice System in a College Town* (New York: Doubleday, 2015), 83.

5. Jonathan Zimmerman, "Blame Football, Not Title IX," *Los Angeles
   Times,* January 9, 2014, at http://articles.latimes.com/2014/jan/
   09/opinion/la-oe-zimmerman-football-title-ix-ncaa-20140109,

accessed January 9, 2016; Judith Shulevitz, "Accused College Rapists Have Rights, Too," *New Republic*, October 11, 2014, at https://newrepublic.com/article/119778/college-sexual-assault-rules-trample-rights-accused-campus-rapists, accessed January 9, 2016; Stuart Taylor Jr. and KC Johnson, "The New Standards for Campus Sexual Assault: Guilty Until Proven Innocent," *National Review* 67 (December 7, 2015): 36–38; "124 Colleges, 40 School Districts under Investigation for Handling of Sexual Assault," *Huffington Post*, July 24, 2015, at http://www.huffingtonpost.com/entry/schools-investigation-sexual-assault_us_55b19b43e4b-0074ba5a40b77, accessed January 8, 2016; Sara Lipka, "An Arc of Outrage," *Chronicle of Higher Education* 61 (April 13, 2015): 26; Jessica Bennett, "Sex, with a Syllabus," *New York Times*, January 10, 2016, p. ST1; Sarah Dunant, "Introduction," in *The War of the Words: The Political Correctness Debate*, ed. Sarah Dunant (London: Virago, 1994), ix; Amanda Hess, "How Drunk Is Too Drunk to Have Sex?" *Slate*, February 11, 2015, at http://www.slate.com/articles/double_x/doublex/2015/02/drunk_sex_on_campus_universities_are_struggling_to_determine_when_intoxicated.html, accessed January 11, 2016.

6. Lipka, "An Arc of Outrage"; Jeannie Suk, "Shutting Down Conversations About Rape at Harvard Law," *New Yorker*, November 11, 2015, at http://www.newyorker.com/news/news-desk/argument-sexual-assault-race-harvard-law-school, accessed January 9, 2016; Margaret Hartmann, "Everything We Know About the UVA Rape Case," *New York Magazine*, July 30, 2015, at http://nymag.com/daily/intelligencer/2014/12/everything-we-know-uva-rape-case.html, accessed January 9, 2016; Emily Yoffe, "The College Rape Overcorrection," *Slate*, December 7, 2014, at http://www.slate.com/articles/double_x/doublex/2014/12/college_rape_campus_sexual_assault_is_a_serious_problem_but_the_efforts.html, accessed January 9, 2016; Shulevitz, "Accused College Rapists Have Rights, Too"; Krakauer, *Missoula*, 343–344; Taylor and Johnson, "The New Standards for Campus Sexual Assault," 36–38.

7. Bailey, "Sexual Revolution(s)," 240; Jonathan Zimmerman, "Let's Drink to Good Grades!," *Pittsburgh Post-Gazette*, September 29, 2013, at http://www.post-gazette.com/opinion/Op-Ed/2013/09/29/Let-s-drink-to-good-grades/stories/201309290102, accessed January 11, 2016; Karen G. Weiss, *Party School: Crime, Campus, and Community* (Boston: Northeastern University Press, 2013), 134–135; Britton White, "Student Rights: From *in loco parentis* to *sine parentibus* and Back Again? Understanding Family Educational Rights and Privacy Act in Higher Education," *Brigham Young University Education and Law Journal* 2007, no. 2 (2007): 330; Heather E. Moore, "University Liability When Students Commit Suicide: Expanding the Scope of the Special Relationship," *Indiana Law Review* 40, no. 2 (2007): 423–424; Mark Oppenheimer, "Person Up, Yale Students," *Tablet*, November 10, 2015, at http://www.tabletmag.com/jewish-news-and-politics/194874/person-up-yale-students, accessed January 10, 2016.

Chapter 6

1. Christopher P. Loss, *Between Citizens and the State: The Politics of American Higher Education in the Twentieth Century* (Princeton, NJ: Princeton University Press, 2011), 20, 42; Jonathan Zimmerman, "*Brown*-ing the American Textbook: History, Psychology, and the Origins of Modern Multiculturalism," *History of Education Quarterly* 44, no. 1 (Spring 2004): 60, 62; Martha Biondi, *The Black Revolution on Campus* (Berkeley: University of California Press, 2012), 20; Elisabeth Lasch-Quinn, *Race Experts: How Racial Etiquette, Sensitivity Training, and New Age Therapy Hijacked the Civil Rights Revolution* (New York: Norton, 2001), 127–132; Andrew Hartman, *A War for the Soul of America: A History of the Culture Wars* (Chicago: University of Chicago Press, 2015), 228.

2. Daniel G. Solorzana, "Critical Race Theory, Race and Gender Microaggressions, and the Experience of Chicana and Chicano Scholars," *Qualitative Studies in Education* 11, no. 1 (1998): 132, 121; "How Unintentional but Insidious Bias Can Be the Most Harmful," *PBS News Hour*, November 13, 2015, at http://www.pbs.org/newshour/

bb/how-unintentional-but-insidious-bias-can-be-the-most-harmful/, accessed January 11, 2016; Derald Wing Sue, *Microaggressions in Everyday Life: Race, Gender, and Sexual Orientation* (New York: John Wiley, 2010), xv, 32–33.

3. Josh Hedtke, "California Professors Instructed Not to Say 'America Is the Land of Opportunity,'" *College Fix*, June 10, 2015, at http://www.thecollegefix.com/post/22839/, accessed December 28, 2015; David Hookstead, "Wisconsin University Dubs 'America Is a Melting Pot' a Racial Microaggression," *College Fix*, June 30, 2015, at http://www.thecollegefix.com/post/23135/, accessed December 28, 2015; Peter Hasson, "UWM Says 'Politically Correct' Is No Longer Politically Correct," *Campus Reform*, October 21, 2015, at http://www.campusreform.org/?ID=6907, accessed December 28, 2015; Emma Pierson and Leah Pierson, "What Do Campus Protesters Really Want?," *New York Times*, December 9, 2015, at http://kristof.blogs.nytimes.com/2015/12/09/what-do-campus-protesters-really-want/, accessed January 24, 2016; Leah Libresco, "Here Are the Demands from Students Protesting Racism at 51 Colleges," *fivethirtyeight.com*, December 3, 2015, at http://fivethirtyeight.com/features/here-are-the-demands-from-students-protesting-racism-at-51-colleges/, accessed January 24, 2016; Scott Jaschik, "Escalating Demands," *Inside Higher Ed*, December 3, 2015, at https://www.insidehighered.com/news/2015/12/03/student-protest-lists-demands-get-longer-and-more-detailed, accessed January 24, 2016; Dani Marrerro Hi, "Viewpoint: 4 Things Not to Do While Celebrating Cinco de Mayo," *USA Today College*, May 4, 2015, at http://college.usatoday.com/2015/05/04/viewpoint-4-ways-to-not-celebrate-cinco-de-mayo/, accessed January 9, 2016; 'Oberlin Students Take Culture War to the Dining Hall," *New York Times*, December 21, 2015, at http://www.nytimes.com/2015/12/22/us/oberlin-takes-culture-war-to-the-dining-hall.html, accessed January 9, 2016; Tina Nguyen, "College Students Demand Culturally Sensitive Cafeteria Food," *Vanity Fair*, December 22, 2015, at http://www.vanityfair.com/news/2015/12/oberlin-protest-dining-hall-food?mbid=social_facebook, accessed January 9, 2016; "When Trigger Warnings

Offend," *Atlantic*, August 27, 2015, at http://www.theatlantic. com/notes/all/2015/08/debating-the-new-campus-pc/402113/ ?oldest=true, accessed January 16, 2016; Greg Lukainoff and Jonathan Haidt, "The Coddling of the American Mind" *Atlantic* 316, no. 2 (September 2015): 42–52.

4. Michael Miller, "Columbia Students Claim Greek Mythology Needs a Trigger Warning," *Washington Post*, May 14, 2015, at https://www.washingtonpost.com/news/morning-mix/wp/ 2015/05/14/columbia-students-claim-greek-mythology-needs-a-trigger-warning/, accessed January 11, 2106; Jenny Jarvie, "Trigger Happy," *New Republic*, March 3, 2014, at https://newrepublic.com/ article/116842/trigger-warnings-have-spread-blogs-college-classes-thats-bad, accessed January 11, 2016; Colleen Flaherty, "Trigger Unhappy," *Inside Higher Ed*, April 14, 2014, at https:// www.insidehighered.com/news/2014/04/14/oberlin-backs-down-trigger-warnings-professors-who-teach-sensitive-material, accessed January 11, 2016; American Association of University Professors, "On trigger warnings," August 2014, at http://www. aaup.org/report/trigger-warnings, accessed January 11, 2016; "What's All This About Trigger Warnings?," National Coalition Against Censorship Report, November 30, 2015, at http://ncac.org/ wp-content/uploads/2015/11/NCAC-TriggerWarningReport.pdf, at http://ncac.org/resource/ncac-report-whats-all-this-about-trigger-warnings, accessed January 11, 2016.

5. Janell Ross, "Obama Says Liberal College Students Should Not Be 'Coddled': Are We Really Surprised?," *Washington Post*, September 15, 2015, at https://www.washingtonpost.com/ news/the-fix/wp/2015/09/15/obama-says-liberal-college-students-should-not-be-coddled-are-we-really-surprised/, accessed January 10, 2016; Robby Soave, "Chicago Students Vow to Destroy 'Hate Speech' as Soon as They Figure Out What It Is," *Reason*, January 13, 2015, at http://reason.com/blog/2015/01/13/ student-newspaper-begs-u-of-chicago-to-c, accessed January 10, 2016; Darlene M. Hantzis and Devoney Looser, "Of Safe(R) Spaces and 'Right' Speech: Feminist, Histories, Loyalties, Theories, and the Dangers of Critique," in *PC Wars: Politics*

and Theory in the Academy, ed. Jeffrey Williams (New York: Routledge, 1995), 227–229; "Protesters Smear Fake Blood on Faces at Blogger Milo Yiannopoulos' Rutgers' Talk," *NJ.com*, February 10, 2016, at http://www.nj.com/middlesex/index.ssf/2016/02/rutgers_students_protest_milo_yiannopoulos_speech.html, accessed February 11, 2106; Elizabeth Redden, "Middle East Conflict, US Campuses," *Inside Higher Ed*, June 17, 2014, at https://www.insidehighered.com/news/2014/06/17/pro-palestinian-student-activism-heats-causing-campus-tensions, accessed January 21, 2016; Lukainoff and Haidt, "The Coddling of the American Mind"; Scott Jaschik, "What the Protests Mean," *Inside Higher Ed*, November 16, 2015, at https://www.insidehighered.com/news/2015/11/16/experts-consider-what-protests-over-racial-tensions-mean, accessed January 24, 2016; Tressie McMillan Cottom, "The Discomfort Zone," *Slate*, December 3, 2013, at http://www.slate.com/articles/life/counter_narrative/2013/12/minneapolis_professor_shannon_gibney_reprimanded_for_talking_about_racism.html, accessed December 28, 2015; Jonathan Zimmerman, "Colleges as Country Clubs," *Los Angeles Times*, April 21, 2013, at http://articles.latimes.com/2013/apr/21/opinion/la-oe-zimmerman-college-luxuries-20130421, accessed January 9, 2016; Caitlin Flanagan, "Today's College Students Can't Take a Joke," *Atlantic* 316, no. 2 (September 2015): 54–59; "What's All This About Trigger Warnings?"; William Deresiewicz, *Excellent Sheep: The Miseducation of the American Elite and the Way to a Meaningful Life* (New York: Free Press, 2014), 42, 22; Arthur Levine and Diane R. Dean, *Generation on a Tightrope: A Portrait of Today's College Student*, 3rd ed. (San Francisco: Jossey-Bass, 2012), xiii, 122; "As the Semester Ends, Students Hold Sit-Ins, Win Higher Pay, and Unionize," *StudentNation*, June 22, 2015, at http://www.thenation.com/article/as-the-semester-ends-students-hold-sit-ins-win-higher-pay-and-unionize/, accessed January 8, 2016; Barbara Ransby, "Students as Moral Teachers: A Survey of Student Activism and Institutional Responses," *Diversity and Democracy* 18, no. 4 (Fall 2015), at https://www.aacu.org/diversitydemocracy/2015/fall/ransby, accessed January 17, 2016; "Fifteen Youth Movements to Dismantle White Supremacy This Summer,"

StudentNation, August 7, 2015, at http://www.thenation.com/article/15-youth-movements-to-dismantle-white-supremacy-rising-this-summer/, accessed January 8, 2016.

Conclusion

1. "Hillary D. Rodham's 1969 student commencement speech," at http://www.wellesley.edu/events/commencement/archives/1969commencement/studentspeech, accessed January 26, 2016; "Senator Edward W. Brook's [sic] commencement address to the Wellesley College class of 1969," at http://www.wellesley.edu/events/commencement/archives/1969commencement/commencementaddress, accessed January 26, 2016.

2. Robert Cohen, "The New Left's Love-Hate Relationship with the University," in *The Port Huron Statement: Sources and Legacies of the New Left's Founding Manifesto,* ed. Richard Flacks and Nelson Lichtenstein (Philadelphia: University of Pennsylvania Press, 2015), 120; Sara Lipka, "An Arc of Outrage," *Chronicle of Higher Education* 61 (April 13, 2015): 26.

3. Andrew Kelly, "The Real Winners in Campus Protests? College Administrators," *Forbes,* November 24, 2015, at http://www.forbes.com/sites/akelly/2015/11/24/the-real-winners-in-campus-protests-college-administrators/#1c27be54c2e4, accessed December 24, 2015; Mark Oppenheimer, "Person Up, Yale Students," *Tablet,* November 10, 2015, at http://www.tabletmag.com/jewish-news-and-politics/194874/person-up-yale-students, accessed January 10, 2016; Helen Horowitz, *Campus Life: Undergraduate Cultures from the End of the Eighteenth Century to the Present* (Chicago: University of Chicago Press, 1988), 229.

4. Jon Wiener, "Barney Frank's 'Stupidest Decision,'" *Nation,* March 20, 2015, at http://www.thenation.com/article/barney-franks-stupidest-decision/, accessed January 20, 2016; James C. Cobb, "The Sad Demise of the Commitment to Free Speech at America's Universities," *History News Network,* December 8, 2015, at http://historynewsnetwork.org/article/161403, accessed January 20, 2016; "Report of the committee on freedom of expression at Yale," December 23, 1974, at http://yalecollege.yale.edu/faculty-staff/

faculty/policies-reports/report-committee-freedom-expression-yale, accessed January 24, 2016.

5. Donald Alexander Downs, *Restoring Free Speech and Liberty on Campus* (Cambridge, UK: Cambridge University Press, 2005), 111; Mary Grigsby, *College Life Through the Eyes of Students* (Albany, NY: SUNY Press, 2009), 85–86.

6. Greg Lukianoff, *Unlearning Liberty: Campus Censorship and the End of American Debate* (New York: Encounter, 2014 [2012]), 253; April Kelly-Woessner, "How Marcuse Made Today's Students Less Tolerant Than Their Parents," *Heterodox Academy*, September 23, 2015, at http://heterodoxacademy.org/2015/09/23/how-marcuse-made-todays-students-less-tolerant-than-their-parents/, accessed January 21, 2016; "College Freshmen Are More Liberal and Keen on Political Activism, Survey Says," *Los Angeles Times*, February 10, 2016, at http://www.latimes.com/local/lanow/la-me-ln-american-freshman-survey-more-liberal-20160210-story.html, accessed February 17, 2016; Arthur Levine and Diane R. Dean, *Generation on a Tightrope: A Portrait of Today's College Student*, 3rd ed. (San Francisco: Jossey-Bass, 2012), 73–77.

7. Greg Lukainoff and Jonathan Haidt, "The Coddling of the American Mind," *Atlantic* 316, no. 2 (September 2015): 42–52; Student Press Law Center, "Newspaper Thefts," at http://www.splc.org/page/newspaper-theft-resources, accessed January 27, 2016; Lukianoff, *Unlearning Liberty*, 224.

8. University of Chicago, "Report of the Committee on Freedom of Expression," 2015, at http://provost.uchicago.edu/FOECommitteeReport.pdf, accessed January 28, 2016.

9. Elizabeth Redden, "Middle East Conflict, US Campuses," *Inside Higher Ed*, June 17, 2014, at https://www.insidehighered.com/news/2014/06/17/pro-palestinian-student-activism-heats-causing-campus-tensions, accessed January 21, 2016; Jonathan Zimmerman, "What Happened to Freedom of Speech?," *Inside Higher Ed*, April 13, 2015, at https://www.insidehighered.com/views/2015/04/13/essay-criticizes-colleges-expelling-students-racist-comments, accessed December 22, 2015.

10. Rosa Ehrenreich, "What Campus Radicals?," in *Beyond PC: Toward a Politics of Understanding*, ed. Patricia Aufderheide (St. Paul, MN: Graywolf, 1992), 136; William Deresiewicz, *Excellent Sheep: The Miseducation of the American Elite and the Way to a Meaningful Life* (New York: Free Press, 2014), 17; Jean M. Twenger, "The Rise of the Self and the Decline of Intellectual and Civic Interest," in *The State of the American Mind*, ed. Mark Bauerlein and Adam Bellow (Conshohocken, PA: Templeton Press, 2015), 129.

11. Levine and Dean, *Generation on a Tightrope*, 126; Lukianoff, *Unlearning Liberty*, 145, 152–153.

INDEX